Mr. Rowe recalled a handsome-looking man from the "Ministry" popping down on his BMW motorbike every-other Friday, - to check how `things` were progressing! Egbert, the first person to use a Rotavator in the West Country, recalls this costing £131. 10s 0d, coming from Mitchell's at Truro. It was a Howard Rotavator, which bolted on the back of a Ferguson Tractor.

"The bottom gear was too high". £337.10 shillings was paid for the Ferguson (petrol) tractor and a two-furrow plough. Petrol was priced at one shilling and thrupence per gallon.

When Egbert, one of eight men working at the airfield during this period, first used the Rotavator, "Men", including the handsome gentleman on the Motorbike and two others driving all the way from Bristol and Launceston in Taxis, came to see him working with the `machine` and marvelled.

1941

April 28th 1941 saw Penzance and the Isles of Scilly attacked by German aircraft. Around this time Hurricane Fighters of 87 Squadron were stationed on St. Mary's, having been transferred from bases on the Cornish mainland to improve their range over the Western Approaches.

On the 3rd June 1941, shortly after 5 p.m. a Dragon Rapide G-ACPY disappeared after taking off from St. Mary's, Isles of Scilly bound for St. Just Airfield with 5 passengers, - the Leggitt family, and the pilot, Captain Anderson – who had completed over 1,000 flights on the Service, on board. Only one body (a passenger) was found, washed up near Portreath. The Service was suspended and resumed 27th October 1941 after it was established that a Heinkel 111H4 of 1/KG28 returning to Nantes following an abortive attack on Barrow-in-Furness where H.M.S. Indomitable was being fitted out, attacked the aircraft. The nose-mounted machine engine caught fire and the DH84 crashed into the sea and sank. It appeared to be a legitimate target from its appearance and government links.

There being a number of radar installations in Penwith, including one on Chapel Carn Brea at that time, GWA worked more closely with the Trevescan Radar Station near Sennen to confirm when the Luftwaffe was about. Ken Olds recalls the throb of German aero engines sounding very sinister to his youthful ear when they were somewhere out over the sea.

During August 1941 telephone reports of a German flying-boot at Praa Sands was mistaken by `Higher Command` for a `Flying-Boat` and brought Officers on a `wild-goose chase`! About this time `window` tin-foil strips were dropped by the R.A.F. over Penwith to prove they could disrupt radar locating aircraft over enemy territory.

The autumn of 1941 saw the arrival of Captain Morris Hearn at Land`s End Airport. Capt. M. E. Hearn, M.B.E., described "as a thickset, blue-eyed, clean-shaven man, fair hair turned grey/white, and, very much his own Boss", was the Chief (and only) Pilot.

Lands End Airfield

He began flying in the R.A.F. in 1919 and when he left in 1941, released from No.10 Bombing and Gunnery School Dumfries, he took up the post at Land's End, for 'Great Western and Southern Air Services Limited. He quickly adopted a remedy against surprise attack by attaching a car mirror to his cockpit canopy to provide him with a rearward view of hostile aircraft.

Captain Hearn's duties meant him flying two daily return trips from Land's End to the I.O.S. (but not on Sundays), ambulance and 'charter' flights. He flew through the War, covering about five thousand return flights. In total, flying sometimes in 'difficult' weather, without the assistance of radio or radar, or Second pilot, he covered approximately three hundred and fifty thousand miles, about a dozen times around the world! Some achievement, since it involved almost endless take-offs and landings and flying duration averaged twenty minutes (either way). The most suitable landing area at St. Just was from east to west, only six hundred and fifty yards, and, from north to south, seven hundred and fifty yards. On the Isles of Scilly at St. Mary's it was about five hundred yards one direction and about six hundred in the other direction.

Captain 'Tubby' Hearn c1940

1942

During 1942 Tregavarah Methodist Chapel twix St. Just and Penzance was destroyed by bombing, never to be replaced. Leslie Oats, brother of Arnold, a former policeman who is renowned for his singing voice, had reluctantly, at their mother's insistence, sang his first and only 'Solo' in the in the Chapel the previous day. He thought his voice had brought the Chapel down!

Other local involvement in war-time included the D.F. and monitoring station at Skewjack, where there was some enemy activity. Holman's Foundry and Gas Works at Tregerseal was bombed. In June Penzance suffered an air raid which left craters.

On the evening of 26th September there was a bombing raid on Penzance. A Dornier 217 of I/KG2 was caught by a Beaufighter from Predannack piloted by Squadron Leader Denis Furze and Pilot Officer John Downes. The Dornier was heading in from the sea and the Beaufighter gave chase, firing until it spiraled downwards, hitting the top of the Wesleyan Sunday School in Cape Cornwall Street and heading up Chapel Road wrecking two cottages. Jack and Lorna Hocking, woken by their cat, 'Nigger' in their Morrison Shelter, saw it coming towards their house up the road.

Images: Dragon Rapide G-ACPP at St Marys, summer 1945

6

The fatalities were amongst the crew but no civilians died on this occasion although an engine bounced down three gardens walls and the Free Church before ending in garden of Noon Gres.

1943

In August, Hurricane II Z3658 of No. 1449 Flight, stationed at Scilly, piloted by Flight Sgt Hunter, was attempted to fly between the masts of the RMS Scillonian `twix Penzance and St. Mary's in order to impress a young lady on board, when the wing of the aircraft hit the fore top mast, and was torn off – the aircraft burst into flames and crashed in the sea. All that were found were papers and parts of the plane. The pilot was killed.

Peter Board of Camborne, Cornwall, recalls when "Stationed" at R.A.F. Portreath with No.1.O.A.D.U, in 1943, a "Bristol Bisley" with engine trouble, landing at St. Just Airfield, and he was sent to sort out the problem, which involved a plug change, and further checks. In July, Dragon GADDI went to Vickers and G-AGIF arrived, serving until March 1944.

`Old Coffins`
(See also `An American Visitor drops in)

In September of that year a B-17 bomber force-landed at the partially obstructed Land's End field. Sixteen aircraft from the 305BG(H) based at Chelveston were dispatched to attack Nantes, France, together with elements of the 91st, 303rd and 306 Bomb Groups on the16th September 1943. The B 17 Bomber "Old Coffins" code XK-J, 305th BG (H), was in the above formation. After a successful mission, with no casualties, the group turned for home.

Around dusk, low on fuel, "Old Coffins" landed at St. Just Airfield, with possible damage to landing gear and propellers. There are reported local sightings of air bags being used to raise the aircraft. [Normal procedure was to underlay with pneumatic jacks and inflate using a compressor] prior to attempting take-off, USAAF mobile repair unit carried out repairs, and, removed all weapons and armour to reduce Aircraft weight. With minimum crew and fuel, "Old Coffins" successfully departed from St. Just 28th September, returning to Chelveston.

Before assignment to the 305th BG (H), "Old Coffins" was assigned to the 381 BG (H) and flown over to the U.K. base at Rodgewell, where she flew fourteen Missions with the 532nd Bomb Squadron - code VE-L. Transferred to the 365th BS/305th BG (H) Code XK-J Chelveston, 22/8/1943.
"Old Coffins" continued in service until returned to the Tinker AAB, USA 23/6/1944, and, after several tours around Amarillo, Keesler, Sheppard AAB`s, the Reclamation Finance Centre at Walnut Ridge took war weary aircraft on 28/12/1945 and sold for meltdown at scrap metal price! A very sad ending.

Lands End Airfield

1944

John Ellis was born in Boscaswell village, near Pendeen, Cornwall in 1922, the son of a mining engineer. Having served in the Royal Navy from 1941 and trained as a Signalman, he was sent to the Patrol Service in Lowestoft, where he joined a flotilla which was engaged in minesweeping & convoy escort in the Western Approaches and the English Channel. In 1942 he sustained severe injuries and burns, consequently invalided out of the Navy. In 1943, he joined GWS (Great Western and Southern Airways) known within the Company as "Gas, Water, and Sewerage".

In the spring of 1944, John was sent to St. Mary's, Isles of Scilly to replace Dennis O Manning, formerly in charge of the Airport, who had moved to the Airline's base at Speke Airport, Liverpool. John remained in Scilly until 1947, when he returned to the mainland and served with BEA (British European Airways), later British Airways, at various other locations, finally retiring in 1977 from BA at Manchester Airport.

Soon they began circling very low – about 50` to 60` over the water. They spotted an object, Working for GWS, John found that his knowledge of signals procedures particularly useful; in that all flight movements had to be authorized by the RAF at Plymouth and sent in code by telephone whenever they needed to fly. John decoded Signals, an easy job compared to deciphering Naval codes! He also "doubled" as a Traffic Assistant, involved with Bookings, compiling load sheets, loading, refueling and, `swinging the props`.

JOHN`S FIRST FLIGHT

One returning from Scilly one morning, Captain Hearn was very excited. "Come on John," he said, "You and I are going mine-sweeping". He had spotted an object floating some distance to the north of the Longships Lighthouse and, knowing John's minesweeping background, asked whether he would be able to identify it. John thought he could, and, since it was in Shipping Lane, and an obvious danger to coastal convoys. He reported it to the Naval Authorities and was given clearance to `take off and search`. which, after very close examination, John confirmed to be a mine. They needed to mark it for destruction by gunfire from a naval torpedo boat based at Newlyn. This marking procedure involved opening the rear door of the aircraft, a Twin-engine DH84. John threw out two smoke canisters which, narrowly missing the mine, gave forth ribbons of red smoke which would mark the site for two hours.

That was John's first flight ever, and very exciting it was, so exciting that he nearly forgot to wind in the trailing radio aerial. Later that day, there was a tremendous explosion to seaward of the Airport. Confirmation of the mine's destruction came in the form of a very polite `Thank you` by telephone from the Senior Navy Officer based in Newlyn. Gordon Stevens was in the ATC stationed at Land`s End during 1943 - 45...then went into the R.A.F. He flew in D.H Rapides and D. H. Dominos from L.E. for the Experience`. He remembered the passenger windows being painted `white` (for black-out).

A Bird's Eye View

SWINGING THE PROPS

This was the recognized procedure used for starting the engines on the DH84 aircraft intended to conserve the aircraft's batteries that supplied the power for the radio equipment and lighting. The Propeller was carefully turned until nearly full compression was reached and then held by the tip of the blade. Next the ignition was switched on and, at a signal from the pilot, the propeller blade tip was pulled smartly in the direction of the rotation when, nine times out of ten, the engine would fire. The same procedure was repeated for the starboard engine.

Later aircraft, such as the DH89A had more powerful engines, and, batteries which absolved John and his Colleagues from this dangerous practice!

AN AMERICAN VISITOR DROPS IN

John Ellis was cycling to the Airport one summer morning at about 0800, when he was staggered to see a B17 Flying Fortress of the USAAF (United States Army Air Force) in the middle of the airfield. There were no runways, only strips of closely mown coarse grass, gorse and heather, and this rather large aircraft was just sitting there, with one landing wheel stuck in a deep depression. Apparently it had been flying over France on a `raid`, been shot up, had lost its way and run out of fuel.

It caused great excitement among the local populace for a day or so, but eventually, not having sustained any great damage on landing, it was lightened of everything possible, including armaments, refueled with the MINIMUM required, and, with a skeleton crew, took off with an almighty ROAR, and disappeared over the cliffs north of Sennen Cove. It re-appeared climbing northward bound for St. Eval Airfield on the North Cornish Coast

Pilots at this time included Capt. `Skipper` Hearn, Capt. George Garland Capt. Brown [on Relief] and Capt. `Tiny` Brown from Sennen -`Tiny` was a very big man – just able to fit into the cockpit!

The Pilot was always the last to embark and often had to apologize as he squeezed his bulk between the Passengers already seated. There was little room in the Hold for anything other than passengers` baggage, but occasionally urgently needed parts for a car, or fishing-boat engines turned up, and were gratefully received at St. Mary's by owners anxious to be under way again.

The Flower-picking season, for which Scilly is famous, usually began in December and reached its peak, in March or April. The bulk of the packed flowers were sent by sea, but on days when there was no sailing, Growers, keen to send `early varieties` to the London market, brought boxes of Soleil d`or and Paper Whites to the Airport.

Lands End Airfield

These were stowed in every available space, even lashed to empty seats. This was quite profitable for the Airline, and, at £16 per box, in the 1944 -45 winters London market, this was `boom time` for the Scillonian growers. On arrival at Land`s End Airport, the flowers were delivered by Bus to Penzance Railway Station for shipping to London.

1945

In May, Germany surrendered. A new charter company was formed, 'Island Air Services' operating two Proctors [G-AHGR and G-AHTF] based on St. Mary's. They were used for pleasure flights and the transportation of flowers and vegetables to Land's End. This company expanded so fast that this operation was wound up for the more lucrative London market in Dec 1948.

Just after World War 2, Warrant Officer C. C. King, was flying a Spitfire back to England from Germany. His first landing was to be at Land`s End Airfield but his compass was defective. He managed to get across Channel and reached the Cornish coast. Because there was thick fog, he inched his way along the coast trying to find a recognizable feature. After some time, flying without success, the fog began to thin and he just managed to spot the airfield below him. He landed but the Spitfire came to rest in a hedge and had to be extracted before it could be moved on.

POST-WAR FLYING, IN WINTER AND SUMMER

The War's end brought back the Holidaymakers, some of who returned year after year, and traffic increased to such an extent that two DH89As were used. The need for a radio operator on board diminished. His absence released another seat; so eight passengers could now be carried. Flights were usually delightful experiences, and schedules were relaxed so that en route little diversions were often made over the outer islands, the Bishop Rock Lighthouse or south of the planned route to fly over a large transatlantic passenger liner such as the Queen Mary or Queen Elizabeth.

Winter flying was quite another matter. Heavy gales, low cloud, snow and ice, often made flying difficult and hazardous, but dedicated Pilots and Ground Staff worked in happy association to provide a link, which has always been appreciated by Scillonian.

Flight duration was scheduled at 20 minutes each way, In the teeth of a 60 mph Westerly gale, it could seem as though the aircraft would never get there – but what a quick ride back to Land`s End, at nearly 180 mph, less 100` above the stormy Atlantic.

1946

1st January, Civil flying was de-restricted. Rapide G-AGUV joined the Great Western and Airlines fleet. By 1946 there were four return services running daily. During this period sixty-five services were cancelled, fifty-two, due to "no Traffic", and, thirteen to weather. This resulted in an average percentage regularity of 80%. Instructions were given to `effect economy` as far as possible in persuading traffic to utilize three of the four services.

A Bird's Eye View

This would seem to account for the fairly high number of services cancelled due to 'no traffic'. The thirteen services cancelled due to weather, indicated the extremely high standard of operation achieved in this area, without direct Radio considering the weather conditions usually experienced at this time of the year.

Various small companies operated on a charter basis over a few years at L.E and St. Mary's. There was also mention of three 'special Charters', which were carried out on behalf of the Isles Of Scilly Steamship Company, for the transportation of Mail, due to the last-minute breakdown of the Steamship that operated between Penzance and the Islands. The freight of nearly 18,000lbs conveyed on those Flights, indicated that the Islanders were reliant on the service as a conveyance of freight to & from the mainland.

Doubling as a garage and a workshop where maintenance and inspections on Aircraft were performed; the original hangar was just large enough to accommodate two De Haviland Rapides (DH89s) and, a couple of cars. Some passengers arrived by car, but most used to arrive at the St. Just Terminal Building, in a small bus hired from Western National (the main Bus Operator). The bus used to wait in the railway station car park at Penzance, the terminus of the railway, since the majority of travellers to the Isles of Scilly made the journey of some three hundred miles or so from London and the Midlands by train.

1947

On the 1st February Great Western and Southern Airlines were taken over by British European Airways (BEA) retaining the Staff and the Rapides Captain Hearn, by this time Airport Manager at Land's End and St. Mary's, joined BEA as a Rapide pilot. Consideration was given to the future of Land's End airfield during 1947. It was thought that a more suitable civil site might be on part of the new RNAS base [Culdrose] being built near Helston, but this plan was not pursued.

The Land's End/ Scillies route then became a B.E.A. Route.
BEA over the years had 50 different Rapides registered to them. Most of these inherited when BEA was formed, and disposed of without entering service. Seven became the "Islander" Class and bore names. These were:

G-AFEZ   Lord Shaftsbury, acquired 1.2.1947, sold to Airviews Ltd.   5.5.1956 having flown 13,239 hour
G-AFRK   Rudyard Kipling, acquired 1.2.1947. sold to Airviews Ltd. 15.5.195 having flown 13,666 hours.
G-AGSH   James Kier Hardy, acquired 1.1.1947, sold to Airviews Ltd. 4.5.1956 Re-acquired 12.21962,
             sold 2.5.1964 having flown 9,572 hours.
G-AHLL   Sir Henry Lawrence, acquired 1.1.1947, written-off St. Just 21.5.1959 having flown 10,747 hours.
G-AJXB   William Gilbert Grace, acquired 17.12.1948, sold to Eagle Aircraft Services Ltd. 25.4.1955 having
             flown 6,248 hours
G-AKZB   Lord Baden Powell, acquired 8.2.1949, written-off 18.12.1961 having flown 8,846 hours.
G-AJCL   Acquired 12.6.1959, sold 2.5.1964 having flown 6,909 hours

Lands End Airfield

1948

Tom Prowse of Trewellard was an engineer at L.EA after the 1939-45 War, serving for 13 enjoyable years. He recalls pilots such as Capt. Jimmy Wade and Capt. Morris Hearn as Senior Pilot on the D.H. Rapide. These men were all `heroes` to the local children.
Cedric Thomas who built the hangar started the St. Just Flight 24F of the ATC which met in the St. Just Drill Hall. Dr. Derrington took this over in 1948.

1949

In 1949 one of Dr. Derrington`s ATC Cadets – Eric Boyns of Bostraze – did so well in his proficiency exam, he was awarded a free flight to Singapore. This was quite an honour for a farmer's son. Both gentlemen still met and reminisce.

1950 RECOLLECTIONS OF FIREMAN JIM PEARCE

In 1950, Jim Pearce moved back to his 'birth-place', St. Mary's, in the Isles of Scilly, and, as he couldn't find suitable employment, worked as a farm-hand until a job became vacant on the Islands Aerodrome, for an airport fireman. He applied, sat an education test, and was taken on as a temporary fireman until he passed the Fireman's Course. As a member of the Ministry of Transport and Civil Aviation Fire Service, Jim attended a six week initial training course at the School at Penfam Moors, Cardiff. On passing the tests, he was confirmed as a Fireman St. Mary's Airport, Scilly was described as "similar to an upended saucer, needing extreme care on approach and departure" by the 'Air Pilot', a Manual for Aviators.

St. Mary's Aerodrome Fire Service had strength of six: one Section Leader [a rank now known as Station Officer], he was in charge, an Irishman ex. Lighthouse-keeper – Paddy Daly. A Leading Fireman, Welsh ex. soldier – David Jones [later to work for the I.S.S.C], four Firemen, with one still to make up-to-strength: Tom Ellis, ex. Tin miner from Geevor

A Bird's Eye View

and Ernie Blythe, a Yorkshire man who had stayed on the Island after his Regiment had gone home. VEHICLES: were ex. WD: a Bedford water-tender capable of producing foam, a large Wheeton tender that had been produced on the Station because of the Ferry of that time could not handle such a load – also capable of foam production, both with medman pumps permanently mounted.

An RAF type ambulance which was used with the Island's medical services, meeting patients from the off-islands on the quay or attending accidents or simply ferrying patients to the Hospital, ,or, from the Hospital to the Aerodrome for transit via, the Dragon Rapide bi-planes to the mainland airport at St. Just. The Fireman also turned-out with the local brigade for fires and incidents in Town or Country. They also carried water in the summer to supply locals with water at a cost of thirty shillings and sixpence for 350 gallons.

One special service attended was to be taken out in a launch with a trailer pump to keep a French crabber afloat until it got into the Harbour. To keep them sustained the seamen regaled the Firemen with cognac through the night and docked just in time to go to work again, as there had to be fire cover for the services operated by the Rapides, SH, RK, and ZB. Senior Pilot Captain Hearn. The Rapides carried six passengers, one Pilot, and operated in pairs. The Firemen had to stand to for the first service every morning, but kept a close watch on all movements. Not many aircraft had tricycle undercarriages and application of the brake had to be done carefully. If there was a gale, three men had to go out onto the airfield and catch the Rapide, hanging one on each wing, and, one over the rear fuselage – a very tiring exercise! Pat Greenlaw put his elbow through the starboard wing doing this, much to the displeasure of Captain Hearn. Having seen one Rapide in, then the firemen had to go out and catch the second one! The Station on St. Mary's was run much as any other in the MCAFS, with daily inspections, availability, and a log book kept. Any incoming flight was logged, and a stand-by for every stranger landing. Drills were also carried out and inspections, very much like any other aerodrome, except the aircraft were tiny!

Jim recalls many incidents, both on St. Mary's and the other Islands. If it happened during flying hours, they had to be back on the airfield in time to stand-to, for the landings/ takes-offs. Out of hours, they had to make their way to the Station at the aerodrome on hearing the siren. It's called a "shout" nowadays, but they used to call it "Bells /down" (pre-American days) Taffy Jones left to become a D.O. at the new Station Gatwick, to be replaced by Pat Greenlaw. Two firemen were taken from Penzance, Jack Sims and John Griffin; the latter did not stay very long.

There were on spate of accidents on landings; Tony Dart, who tipped a Rapide on its nose while landing on runway 33. Jim remembers speaking to him as they ran-out hoses and got foam on. It seemed odd to talk to this man in his cock-pit, three feet from ground level, while someone went to get the ladder to release his passengers, behind and above him. They eventually lassoed the aft end of the fuselage with a rope, and, brought the tail down with a bang!

13

Lands End Airfield

The nose was straightened out enough to fly back to St. Just Airport, minus the passengers! A little while after, when Income tax came to the islands, the same thing happened, this time with Reporters on board. A Gemini went off 28 Runway whilst taxing. The Pilot Philip Cleiffe later was to have a nastier accident.

A new appliance arrived, a Thorny Croft Foam CO/Tender, which was far too big for the Island, and, was withdrawn to be taken back by landing-craft off Porth Mellon Beach. Unfortunately, the powers that be, had not reckoned on the tide coming in! The vehicle bogged down and was flooded, and, was replaced by two original RAF Bedford's.

An unexploded bomb was discovered at Land's End, thought to have been dropped in 1941. In the 50s and 60s Bernard Paul used to fly radio-control planes [single channel flying].

1951

In 1951, the D.H. Heron prototype G-ALZL visited St. Just Airport and The Scillies.
Olley Air Service had an agreement with BEA. The route linked Croyden, Bristol, Exeter, Newquay and Land`s End – it lasted for one year. Captain G. Chippindall was a pilot employed by British European Airways. About mid May 1951 he was posted to Land's End to operate the Land's End-Scilly Shuttle. Captain "Tubby" Hearn was in charge of the Flight Operations. After "Tubby" Hearn had familiarised Captain Chippindall with the 'peculiarities' of landing and taking-off from both Airfields, he was let loose on the unsuspecting Public!

In those days B.E.A operated two D.H.Rapides daily, to and fro, the Scillies. The two Pilots flew, weather permitting, six round trips daily - approximately. 4.00 hours. Capt Chippindall's log-book shows that the number of flights he operated daily, varied considerably each month, his heaviest month of 'flying', was August 1951 when he flew 85.30 hours. He generally found life was very pleasant, plenty of time to explore Cornwall, enjoyed bringing up his first-born son, who unfortunately can't remember Cornwall at all! Apart from the daily routine of Land's End/Scilly flying, he occasionally was called out for 'Ambulance Charters'. These were generally to bring expectant mothers from the Scillies to the mainland to give birth.

Images Left: Swanpool Beach, Falmouth 1952, Right: St Ives

A Bird's Eye View

1952 "FLYING ENTERPRISE"

The ship "Flying Enterprise" had problems in the Atlantic. Harry Penhaul, a photographer with the Express Newspaper, chartered a Rapide, flown by Captain G. Chippindall, a Pilot who was employed by B.E.A., on the 11th January 1952. Penhaul, [who had a photography shop displaying all his latest snapshots in Market Jew Street, Penzance, not far from the Humphrey Davy Statue] had a `scoop` with the National Press with his photos. The 'Enterprise' was towed into Falmouth with the Captain Henrik Kurt Carlsen still aboard.

Murray Chown, in 1952, used Rapide G-AIYP and charged 10/- (ten shillings - about 50pence) for a "Joy Flight" around the lighthouse.

TRIPPERS

Peter and Mavis Nevin of Croyden, Surrey, drove from Lynmouth, to take their first "Joy Flight" – a scenic flight from St. Just around Land`s End, on 20th August 1952. The small Auster, in which they flew, was a product of the Taylorcraft Aviation Company, founded in 1936. Early models were imported in small quantity and The Taylor Aircraft Co. (England) was established in 1938 to build the Auster under licence - some 1,600 being produced. The Auster was first in action during the invasion of Algeria, proving itself in the Italian campaign and the Western Front, the Netherlands Air Force, and the RCAF also used it. This Auster was, Mavis remembers, still in its Army Livery.

Images: Gliding operations at the airfield.

15

Lands End Airfield

Sheila and John Maynard, originally of London, now residing near Penzance, in August 1952 took a flight from St. Just Airfield to St. Mary's, I.O.S. They were enjoying a holiday in the South West travelling on a `Royal Blue Coach`, stopping off at Yeovil, then Falmouth.

Notes from their diary at that time read: "Moved to digs at Falmouth. Afternoon to Penzance, Land`s End - tea for two people -4/- "Joy Flight" 10/-: to St Ives - coffee for two people -2/- used .2 gals. Petrol. Very fine weather". Twelve years on, the couple took another scenic trip, this time in a D.H.Rapide. Mavis recalls the Pilot, who was very causally dressed, coming out of the hangar, shouting "Let's go" - which they did! They flew over Longships and along the coast. Peter recalls the terminal building, "like a shed", where people booked tickets and drank "burning hot tea!" In the 1990s the couple flew to the Isles of Scilly in an "Islander" and has been continuing this annual holiday since.

The couple sent a postcard, saying: `The showers haven't stopped us going out. Been to Boscastle in North Cornwall, lovely time on the beach; Going to the Inn tonight. Will think of you next Tuesday we are going to the Scilly Isles by Aeroplane. We had a job trying to persuade Mum to go but we're booked now so she can't drop out!` to their relatives from Swanpool Beach. A card sent from Porthcressa, St. Mary's, and I.O.S. read: `It was quite an experience coming here. One day we'll bring you `. Images above : The Maynard family arriving and boarding their flight to St Mary's , Scillies. 1952

Melba Airways
Manchester based Melba Airways, secured a scheduled route between Bournemouth and Land's End from BEA. It ran for just one season as the company went into liquidation. Olley Air Services also secured an agreement with BEA. The route linked Croydon, Bristol, Exeter, Newquay and Land's End. It also lasted for one season.

A Bird's Eye View

SEA FURIES 1950'S

On 26th September 1952 a "Sea Fury" FB11 serial number TF 959 from 738 Squadron Culdrose (Coding 109/CW) suffered engine failure just over the sea, north of Land's End. The Pilot, Sub. Lieutenant Vic Cooke of the Royal Naval Reserves attempted landing at St. Just Airfield and crashed 25 yards off end of runway. Spun in from 5oo feet, crashed, exploded and caught fire over Brea Vean Farm - the Pilot was killed. The engine had seized.

1953

BEA's service was proving very popular and was now well established. During the 1953 season, 36,000 people were carried, with over 50 tons of freight and 12 tons of mail. The Company's virtual monopoly of internal air routes had been revoked in 1953, but, it was 1961 before rivalry to their L.E. – I.O.S Service would emerge: Mayflower, Westpoint, Bardock Aviation and Scillonian Air Services to name but a few. None of them creating much opposition for BEA who ordered two Sikorsky S-6IN helicopters to replace the Rapides in August.1963

1955

Early in the second half of the twentieth century an aircraft direction beacon was erected alongside the Old North Road from Tregerest to Pendeen helping aircraft navigate to and from the Atlantic Crossing.

1956

By 1956, the Rapide fleet on the route was reduced to three. An unusual method of landing in conditions of poor visibility was developed at Land's End, borne of necessity because of the erratic climate and lack of landing aids. Aircraft approaching from St. Mary's would fly to the Brisons Rock off Cape Cornwall then turn east-south-east and descend below the ceiling, travelling along the Cot Valley. Soon after passing over Kelynack Farm and crossing the St. Just-Sennen road two telegraph poles were seen, painted in bold red-and-white stripes. The aircraft would turn sharp right at that point, re-cross the road and drop onto the airfield. The remains of the red-and-white paint have just survived and can be still seen.

David Pitman recalls this procedure whilst training in 1993 on an instrument flight. Staff and friends became concerned when his Cessna 152 did not return from a navigation flight following bad weather across the field. Then suddenly they appeared from nowhere in front of the clubhouse. "We tracked the Lands End VOR (radio Beacon near Pendeen) and tracked out on the 270 radial. Then did a let down through the cloud to find the Brisons underneath us. Colin Shaw then directed me to fly up the Cot valley just at hilltop height

Lands End Airfield

and turn sharp right when the two striped posts came into view. A quick flaps down, flare, brakes and there we were parked in front of the club!

1957

Bookings on route could be made with Messrs. Treglown [Penzance Booking Agent by or the Airport by telephone: St. Just 60 or 79. Ticket prices were now £1.10s 0d single, £2.10s 0d return. The route was said to be BEA's busiest internal flight at the time. Up to 20 round trips a day were made. It was also the last BEA service to operate Rapides. Altogether Rapides G-AFEZ, G-AGSH, G-AHKU, G-AHLL, G-AHXW, G-AJCL and G-AKZB flew on the service over the years.

Janis Byott (formerly from Wolverhampton, but now residing at Porthcurno) recalls that when she was eighteen years old, she took her first flight from St. Just Airport. Janis remembers a small charabanc picking people up from Penzance Railway Station, where there was very little in the way of facilities for the public – just chairs! and taking them to the airfield for a `trip of a life- time`!

It was March, the weather poor. Janis was told by a "Uniform" three times that they did not know if they would, in fact, fly. If they did, it would be at their own risk! So, at first, she was naturally too scared to climb down from the Charabanc. When she alighted, she found, to her surprise, that they had to be weighed with any baggage (nothing much has changed!) The "Uniform" guessed her weight correctly. The flight was superb and Janis has flown frequently since. She said, "It gets better every time!" She also recalls, Anthony Thorn, the author of "Baby and the Battleship" being aboard the charabanc, but cannot remember if he flew!

G-AGSH at Bournemouth Airport 2001

1958

Just three Rapides were now flying the route; G-AHKU 'Cecil John Rhodes', G-AHLL 'Sir Henry Lawrence' and G-AKZB 'Lord Baden Powell'.

Joyce and David Bentley on their Honeymoon flew in a DH Rapide to the Scillies and stayed in the "Star Castle" on St. Mary's. Joyce remembers that she was wearing a hooped skirt, and, had great difficulty in sitting, when the aircraft was parked! They still fly to the Islands from Land's End Aerodrome today! BEA advertisements in The Official Information Bureau at 104 Market Jew Street, Penzance read: `The Scilly Isles – 20 minutes away!

A Bird's Eye View

BEA operates frequent, regular flights between Cornwall and the Isles of Scilly all the year round. Details and bookings from your Travel Agent or BEA, The Airport, St. Just [Telephone: St. Just 79]. The Ministry of transport and Civil Aviation issued a booklet of Emergency Orders for Land`s End [St. Just] Aerodrome on 1st November 1958. The orders were for instruction and guidance of all Services concerned in the event of aircraft accident or emergency. Headings: Aircraft accidents/emergency/fires – action by ATO; AFS. Emergency standby points/Rendezvous points/ Grid map system etc.

Doctors on call:
Dr. Campbell – Tel St. Just 6   Dr. Brewer   - Tel St. Just 6
West Cornwall Hospital Tel. Penzance 2382   Local Police: Tel St. Just 20
Ministers of Religion:
Rev Barrie [C of E] Tel St Just 2172   Rev. Balment Tel. Penzance 2619
Rev. W. Trinder Tel. St. Just 10   Rev. Williams Tel. St. Just 106

1959

The L.E. – St. Mary's Service was the last BEA Route to operate De Havilland Rapides, those in Scotland having been pensioned off in 1955, an, the Channel Islands in 1956. In May 1959 and December 1961 – two Rapides* were lost to the Service due to landing mishaps at Land`s End Airport – there being no injuries on board. On the 21st May Rapide* G-AHLL crashed – written-off- at Land's End when it over-ran and clattered into a Cornish hedge. It was replaced by Rapide G-AJCL from Cambrian Airways.

1960s

In the early 1960s there was a Dock Strike in Penzance and the Scillonian could not sail. Extra flights were made to take supplies to the Scilly Isles. On day alone the planes carried two tons of milk, bread, sugar, flour and meat. June1960, John Chaffey of Bristol enjoyed a short, but interesting flight on a perfect sunny day from St. Just Aerodrome to St. Mary's, on the Isles of Scilly

1961

B.E.A still used De Haviland Rapides to and from the Isles of Scilly. The DH 89 [with 'tapered wings'] and. G-AGSH and G-AJCL. There were four pilots, four Traffic Staff, and five Engineers, and the Firemen doubling as baggage handlers! Summer services were hourly on Saturdays from 0800 - 1900 and eight or nine flights, weekdays. One aircraft operated the schedule, with one on standby and one in Jersey for maintenance.

Bookings were handled in a small office in Wharf Street, Penzance, with two sales officers, including Ron Rogers. The Station Supt. was Geoffrey Waite. Rapide G-AKZB was lost on the 12th December 1961. As it approached Land`s End in foggy conditions the Rapide unfortunately struck a fencing post on the airfield boundary during an attempt at landing. No one was hurt but the plane was written off.

Lands End Airfield

1962

Steven Morrison flew from Lands End Airfield to St. Mary's, in 1962. At that time, British European Airways had a fleet of De Haviland 92A Rapides. Each Rapide had seven Passenger seats. Steven was told that the eighth seat had been removed to allow room for the Royal Mail Transit. The Royal Mail `post horn` logo was part of the Rapides livery, the logo being placed on the aircraft's fin. He recalls that the take-off was the most interesting for him. The wind direction must have been about south-east, with the Rapide going into `take-off run`, without any `hold` at the airfields perimeter, taking-off, approximately parallel with the main Airport Buildings.

It was noteworthy, that the tail of the Rapide lifted almost immediately the `take-off run` begun. Landing at Scilly was interesting as the approach appeared to be at low level, and up-hill to the landing area. Steven was completely deaf for about twenty minutes after landing, due to the sudden descent. He recalls that it was super flying weather, both there and back. "A Fine introduction to passenger flying!"

1962 was the 25th Anniversary of Scheduled Services. During that year, the B.E.A. Helicopter Experimental Unit evaluated the Boeing Vertol BV107, Bristol 192, and, Sikorsky S61, as possible replacements for the Rapides. The S61 was chosen, and, on 1st August 1963, BEA ordered two, one for the Scillies schedule, and one for charter work.

Captain Hearn retired in March as BEA's Senior Pilot at Land's End after nearly twenty years service. During that time he logged 31,560 flights, more than a million miles and some 15,000 hours on the route and had only stayed overnight at St. Mary's on four occasions. He had flown many times in very poor conditions in order for Islanders to receive urgent medical attention on the mainland. He was remembered with great affection.

1963

During the summer of 1963, a Westland Sikorsky WS55, G-AOCF, was based at St. Just, to evaluate the Decca Flight Log Navigation system.

Increasing competition from other airlines [since BEA's virtual monopoly was revoked] began to appear. These airlines used airports further up-country putting pressure on the BEA's Land's End route. These included Mayflower Air Services (Plymouth), Scillonia Air Services [Gatwick], Bardock Aviation [Staverton], British Westpoint Aviation (Exeter) and Solair Flying Services [Coventry]. Due to the increased competition and the fact that the Rapides were now showing their age, the helicopters seemed the best option. They could also carry three times as many passengers and they suited the short runways on St. Mary's – the major reason the Rapides were still being used on the route [because there were very few fixed wing passenger aircraft that could operate from such short distances].

A Bird's Eye View

'Changeover day' from Rapides to Sikorsky S61s

1964

The following year, the Rapides finished on Friday 1st May and the next day the S.61 N helicopters purchased from United Aircraft International took their place. It was planned to use just one of the two purchased for purely financial reasons. Although originally 26 seater, they now carried 28, fully amphibious, powered by two General Electric T58-110 engines. They were `Crewed` by a Captain, First Officer and Cabin Attendant. Both of BEA's helicopters, G-ASNL and G-ASNM, departed Land's End for St. Mary's. G-ASNL, piloted by Captain Jock A Cameron [Manager Helicopter Unit] flew the first scheduled flight the next day. A heliport in Penzance was planned and a site at Eastern Green was selected. BEA left Land's End airfield and the Land's End Aero Club, now managed the aerodrome, keeping the site financially intact. Helicopter Unit flew G-ASNL.

The Rapides which had been in use by BEA since 1947 were sold to WestPoint Airlines, and the last scheduled B.E.A. Rapide passenger service, flown by Captain Ron Hurcombe, left St. Mary's, Isles of Scilly, at 16. 30 hours, arriving back at St. Just on the mainland, just twenty minutes later. The final commercial flight on that Friday, with Rapides, was an Ambulance Charter G-AJCL.

There were very strong winds and later that evening at the Celebration Party, Captain Hurcombe complained how tired his arms and legs were, trying to control the small aircraft in the high winds. On the same day a Viscount, along with Senior Staff and Reporters came to St. Mawgan to celebrate this event.

On the 1st May both of BEA's helicopters, G-ASNL and G-ASNM, departed Land's End for St. Mary's. G-ASNL flew the first scheduled flight the next day. A heliport in Penzance was planned and a site at Eastern Green was selected. BEA left Land's End airfield and the Land's End Aero Club, established by Viv Bellamy, now managed the aerodrome, keeping the site financially intact.

Lands End Airfield
LAND'S END GLIDING AND FLYING CLUB

With the inauguration of a Helicopter service from Penzance to the Scilly Islands, Land's End Airport, formerly the Terminal for the fixed-wing air service, was closed for commercial aviation, there arose the possibility of forming a Gliding and Flying Club to operate from the Airfield. After careful examination, it was concluded that such a Club could be successfully established provided that:
(a) Security of tenure of buildings, or Permission to erect Club buildings were obtained.
(b) Finances were based on residential holiday gliding courses for Country Members
(c) Full-time instructional staff was available
(d) Power flying and commercial facilities were available.

Having established these basic requirements, enquiries and discussions were initiated, and pertinent information assembled, so that a detailed plan could be drawn up for Guidance should the site become available. So the Club evolved, started by Dave Treadwell from Cable and Wireless, Richard Barns from Lamorna, Dr. Farnell, Principal of Camborne Technical College, David Bath, Tom Blevins of Cable and Wireless.

The site consisted of a small grass airfield with unobstructed approaches, set in open country, about 1,400 yards inland from sea cliffs, facing WSW. The airfield was large enough to permit satisfactory winch or aero-tow launching for gliders in any condition or direction of wind. The sea cliffs offered good prospects for soaring and if the possibility of aero-towing to the cliffs, with a possible field landing was accepted, there were cliffs suitable for soaring in any wind direction within 6 miles of the airfield. Nothing at that time was known about the prospects for thermal or Wave soaring from the site, but active cumulus was frequently observed developing into powerful streets in SW winds, and large lenticulars were observed on occasions. Therefore, the adventurous group decided that there were distinct prospects of advanced soaring being available.

The site was very suitable for power flight training, and was sufficiently large for the two facilities to operate together. Considerate interest was shown in that side of the project as no other training facilities existed nearer than Plymouth. In addition, there was the need in the area for facilities for private aircraft and casual traffic. The Club could provide these.

The main Building, formerly the Passenger Terminal, was of wooden construction, and thought to be readily convertible to residential Club accommodation.

A Bird's Eye View

This had considerable potential for development of social activities, with catering, lounge, and bar facilities available. A brick-built M.T. garage, with two small rooms attached was in good condition. A three-bay fire appliance garage made an excellent workshop for glider maintenance and repairs. The attached offices were suitable for the C.F.I's office, a link Trainer, and a useful store.

Starter battery in Pram

The main hangar would provide adequate accommodation for several gliders and light aircraft, and also stores accommodation but it was in poor condition and needed repair. It was understood that the Ministry had this in hand. More membership potential: Two general classes of Member were envisaged – Local and Country. Local Members would be `those living in the area who flew at weekends and other spare time`. Country Members were `those who joined the Club temporarily specifically for gliding Courses`.

The Resident C.F.I. & Manager was G. Wass, M.A. As Hon. Secretary, Mr. W.D.; Treadwell applied for a Club Registration Certificate to the Magistrates Court in respect of the Annex to the Passenger Lounge, Building No. 3, Land`s End, [St. Just] Airport on 9th October 1965. The aeroplanes they used were: Blanik Czech Glider, Slingsby`s T21 and T31 gliders, Auster 6a [G-ARKE] which was also used as Glider-tug, and, a pre-War Slingsby Skylark [single-seater glider]. There was one hangar fronting the road. The CFI [Certified Flying Instructor] being Jeff Vass. Dr. Keith Reid kept an aeroplane at the airfield. He also carried out the pilot medical inspections.

1965 SCILLONIA AIRWAYS

A new airline, Scillonia Airways, was formed by Captain Brian Neeley, a former Airline Pilot who decided that he would like to run an Airline of his own. Brian came down to Cornwall and rented the St. Just Airfield from the Board of Trade, the start of `Scillonia Airways`. He launched it with a borrowed Rapide aircraft, a £28

overdraft and an `old pram` - a vital piece of equipment for ferrying heavy-duty batteries across the airfield to the aircraft.

This Service linked the RAF St. Mawgan to the Isles of Scilly. He then decided to begin `Scenic Flights` over the spectacular Land`s End Peninsular, with the fare-paying passengers eating buns! Crayfish and lobsters were added to the list of passengers, for Capt. Neely discovered a need for an Air Freight service taking crayfish from Ireland and

23

Lands End Airfield

Cornwall to Brittany, France [just a hundred miles away] where they were in heavy demand. Soon he was sending out about 600 tons of fresh crustaceans per year.

The Crayfish/lobsters were kept in fresh water in a disused `inspection pit` in the `Terminal Building`. These two combined services soon proved to be a problem - As Captain Neeley discovered.

The company acquired Rapides G-ALGC `Bishop`, G-AHAG `Bryher`, G-AHGC `Tresco`, G-AJCL `Samson` and `G-AHKU` a second Bishop`. An order was placed for two Islanders, but this was cancelled before delivery.

Image: Chris Unitt in the Dragon Rapide

Fellow pilots, included Charlie Vaughan and Peter Wootton – who also built the `Tower` and the arch in the Café area. Peter also installed the large window in the lower Café. Other pilots flew in their `time-off` from a major airline.

Richard Marnes's Miles Messenger

1966
Scillonia commenced its first scheduled service between Newquay, Land`s End and St. Mary's in June, while pleasure flights were also undertaken, generally from Land`s End but also from Perranporth.

1968
Scillonia was the last major commercial operator in Europe to use the Rapide aircraft on scheduled routes. However Captain Neely recognized they would need replacing.

Brian Neely and passengers

Joy Flight over the Minack, Porthcurno. 1967

24

A Bird's Eye View

PLEASURE FLIGHT:

Nick and Mary [nee Elliott] Hayes, now residing in an eighteenth century Guest House in Phillack, Hayle, Cornwall, were on holiday in the West Country near Penlee Quarry when they spotted a `Pleasure Flight` aircraft circling overhead. Being interested in old aircraft and vehicles, they decided to investigate, heading to St. Just Airfield where they embarked on a magical scenic trip around West Penwith. Nick recalls the Canadian Pilot sitting `with his feet up on the dash-board` of the aircraft!

On October 31st, BEA's helicopter GAWFX force-landed at Long Rock after a fault occurred crushing its port undercarriage leg. Further faults were found on other S-61`s.

1969

The Penzance helicopter service was suspended in January following further investigation of the fault that occurred on 31st October 1968. BEA borrowed an Islander from Aurigny Air Services to fly their passengers from Land`s End. The helicopter service was back in operation by March but Islander aircraft from Land`s End were used several times in the following years.

AUGUST 1969

Holiday-makers the West family from Devon enjoying a trip on a D H Rapide from St. Just Aerodrome

On Monday 18th August 1969, Miss Elizabeth Taylor, endured a series of delays, mostly due to foggy weather, on her journey to Land`s End, where she greeted twenty-one year old polio victim, David Ryder of Battersea, after his marathon walk from John` Groats-to-Land`s End [861 miles].

Unfortunately, due to work commitments, Richard Burton - Elizabeth Taylor's husband, was unable to accompany his wife and step-daughter, twelve year old, Liza Todd.

The first delay [an hour] was at Heathrow, then at St Mawgan [45 mins.] waiting for transport to arrive – couldn't fly to Land`s End as planned due to fog. Captain Brian Neely, of St. Just [LEA] Airport, drove the car in which she eventually arrived at Land`s End. The first car having sprung a radiator leak was `last straw` said Miss Taylor.

Images:
Elizabeth Taylor with Capt. Brian Neely [on right]
Opening the new Terminal at St. Just Airport

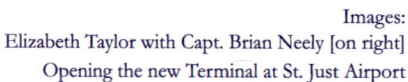

25

Lands End Airfield

The Civic officials waiting at Land's End Airport followed behind as the cavalcade streamed into its destination.

During this visit Elizabeth Taylor also opened the new Terminal at St. Just Airport. Previously the building was used as the 'fire-engine' shed. What was once a very large inspection pit - with steps leading down to the bottom of a very deep pit- converted to a 'holding-tank' for crayfish and lobsters which Brian flew to 'buyers' on the Continent. A Blacksmith from Kelynack made a large metal 'dolly' that was suspended over the 'tank/storage/pond'. On this were many sub-tropical plants. Adorning the outer walls of the building were banana trees and the like. This area was later used as a Café/waiting area.

Elizabeth Taylor with Capt. Brian Neely [on right] Opening the new Terminal at St. Just Airport

In October 1969 Captain B. Neely travelled to Kuwait with the intention of purchasing two Twin Pioneers to replace the Rapides. Unfortunately Scillonia's financial position deteriorated and the purchase was never made.

1970

W.H.LANE & SON of Morrab Road, Penzance, were instructed to sell by Auction at Land's End Airport, St. Just-in-Penwith, on Saturday May 2nd 1970 at 11 a.m. "prompt" items seized under a writ of 'Fi Fa' [fieri facias, usually abbreviated fi. fa. Latin for that you cause to be made] is a writ of execution after judgment obtained in legal action for a debt or damages] and directed to the High Sheriff of Cornwall.

The 'Auction'

David Channel was farming in Truro at the time of the Auction, the 'sale of the entire Contents' of the Airfield. The owner, Brian Neely, a former B.O.A.C Senior First Officer, was unable to pay a loan of a few hundred pounds, for he was in a Kuwait gaol for allegedly flying whiskey through a prohibited area, hence the 'Sale', conducted by Mr. Thurston Lane, Auctioneer.

David set off from Truro very early as there was a 'thick fog', 'so thick in fact, between Redruth and Camborne he had a small accident with another car, but it was not bad enough to stop him continuing his journey. Eventually he arrived at a gate where a large notice told him that he had arrived at the Headquarters of Scillonia Airways. There were three other cars in the car park, and David thought he had made a mistake with the date of the 'Sale'.

A Bird's Eye View

The reason for so few people of course, was due to the dense fog. Most people lost their way or gave up all together, or, thought the `Sale` would have been cancelled. When the Sale` started, there were only about ten or twelve people at the most, and they all came from close by. First of all the aeroplanes were sold, starting with a Rapide which was having a new piece of fabric put on the wing Apart from that, it was perfect, complete with radio communication and everything! It was sold for less than one hundred pounds. The other two Rapides, which were ready to fly, complete with `certification` made less than Two hundred pounds. G-HAGG was purchased by Mr. David Toms - being restored by its new owner. Other items included: Bedford 4 x 4 900 fuel bowser; Austin fire tender with Coventry Climax water pump and fire/rescue equipment and approx 1,000 gallons 100 octane petrol. This being a `Bankruptcy` sale, nothing could be withdrawn, and, David said that they all looked at each other in amazement at the give-away prices.

David came away with the Airport flags, bought for his children. He still has one, in perfect condition - a large flag, in pale blue, on which appear the words "Scillonia Airways" One day it is his intention to present it to the airport.

A pair of large ornamental wrought iron gates, once in the Terminal building, was sold to a Mr. Harold Jackson of `Jackson Antiques` Market Jew Street, Penzance. It is believed that the purchaser had them made into two pairs, a pair of which still can be seen at his old home in Newlyn.

The news of the Airline being sold off to pay a debt reached the National Press, with a Reporter from the Sunday Telegraph writing that "A British pilot serving a year's imprisonment in Kuwait for attempted whisky smuggling is to be told by British Embassy officials tomorrow that the airline he built up was sold for £1,299 at a forced sale yesterday to meet a debt. Friends thought the news would be a "Terrible blow" to Mr. Neely, 44, whose Scillonia Airline at St. Just Airport, near Penzance, Cornwall, was auctioned to satisfy a £1,400 bill. The money is owed to a St. Ives doctor and amateur pilot, Dr. Keith Read who was at the sale. Dr. Read said, "I deeply regret doing this but what is the alternative – just say goodbye to the money? I gave Brian a cheque for a 10-day period so that he could take a petrol delivery and he has not paid me back." While the auction was being held, a letter written by Mr. Neely in his prison cell reached his friend Mr. Michael Reynolds, 30 of Penzance. It authorised him to negotiate payment of the debt. No Help. But Mr Neely protested at service of the writ which forced the sale. I am held incommunicado and quite unable to either move or make contact with any legal representative or indeed speak English to get help from any quarter," he wrote. A Bidder at the sale was Mr. Howard Fry, Liberal parliamentary candidate for St. Ives, who runs Westward Airways, an airline operating in the West Country.; strenuous efforts are being made by the British Ambassador to obtain clemency for Mr. Neely from the Ruler of Kuwait".

Lands End Airfield

Mr. Brian Neely was freed, following pressure from the Foreign Office, after serving six months of a one year sentence in Kuwait for allegedly flying whisky through a prohibited area in Kuwait. He said he would ask the government for a full investigation of his case.

According to local Press, he was arrested in Kuwait having flown to the Middle East to bring home two replacement aircraft he had bought from Kuwait Airways. As a favour for some Americans with whom he had become friendly he was carrying whisky. The Americans staffed the Saudi Arabian pipeline. He had bought the whisky openly in Bahrein, not intended anything illegal. The trial had been a `farce` - the case conducted in Arabic. The `writs` announcing the `break-up were pushed through his cell door. ` Brian said `I came back to England to find my airline had been sold over my head to satisfy a short-term loan of a few hundred pounds which could have been settled on my return.` Whilst `away` his lease on St. Just airfield was terminated and his London home stripped by intruders. It seemed incredible that this could happen under English law while he was held in a foreign prison. He had broken no English laws and had an `impeccable` private and business record. He said hat he had not been ill treated in prison, but had shared a cell with five Arabs who could not speak English`.

Letters in support of Brian Neely from local residents were sent the newspapers protesting that `anybody could buy up his property and take over the fruits of his work while he himself was helpless overseas. This seemed to lack both justice and compassion. If those who took over the airline cannot make a success of it, then justice and compassion, as well as commercial good sense, would suggest that it should go back to Mr. Neely who has shown that he can make a success of it.` voiced many.

The Board of Trade sold the airfield to the local authority – the joint Councils of St. Just, Penzance, St. Ives, County Council and Kerrier District Council. The Aerodrome was now managed by a Joint Committee. It was jointly owned by Penwith District Council (50%), Kerrier District Council (25%) and Cornwall County Council (25%). They, in turn granted a seven-year lease for its operation to Westward [Land`s End] Ltd, [Directors included: Geoff Tregoning and Howard Fry], an associated company of Westward Airways who operated Britten-Norman Islanders, which became the definitive replacement for the Rapides, around the south-west of England, the Isles of Scilly and hauled lobster over to Brittany. Unfortunately there was an incident on the Scillies in 1970 where the aeroplane went through the hedge shortly after it started. The operation ceased.

A Bird's Eye View

During the summer a new company, Island Air Charter, had been formed at Land's End with Islander G-AYCV. This was used for charter work, pleasure flights and the transport of perishables.

By September, Brymon Aviation, which had been formed at Fairoaks during 1969, carried out charter flights in their first Islander, G-AXXJ, to, amongst other places, Land's End and St. Mary's. The Britten-Norman Islander became the definitive replacement for the Rapide. Westward Airways operated this during 1969 and 1970.

Therefore the Airfield at Land's End was basically unused not operated, so the "lease" came up again. Viv Bellamy bought shares in Westward Airways and eventually became Managing Director. Geoffrey Tregonning, Howard Fry and Joe Furniss were still involved in the company. Eventually Viv Bellamy bought the others out.

The `Parkers`, referred to as 'the local Mafia` by Viv Bellamy, had the concession on the Cafe. Eric Parker was also a Civil Aviation `approved` welder. Cessna 172 came from Cameroon G-YOD and at the same time, bought a Rapide (G- AYCR) which cost one thousand Quid. A local engineer worked on it and obtained its C of A. Pay the money and they come down.... Set procedure ...fill a form out.... send the money...and then you are in the system and they come down and carry out the "Inspections". Civil Aviation Inspectors performed these or Licensed Engineers approved by the C.A.A.

There was only one instructor at that time, Peter Assinder. . One of his successful pupils was Mr. Eric Watson, once a member of the `Tortoise Group` (Rod Bellamy, Jeff Bold, Eric Watson) their shared aircraft was a Cessna 150 G-ATOD (1985-2001). After crashing at Bodmin, it was brought to Land's End Aerodrome where it was rebuilt. Eric also flew with Viv Bellamy

Hugh Scanlan, a former Editor of "Shell Aviation Magazine" was a visitor from Penzance and used to fly the Rapide with the permission of Mr. V. Bellamy. Roderick Bellamy, Vivian's son recalls his Father doing the pleasure flying himself. It all seemed `terribly romantic`, just landing into the wind. You didn't have the rules and regulations, or the expertise that you have now, or, for that matter the restrictions on hours. You could fly seven-days-a-week!

Image: Viv Bellamy and Tri-plane

Lands End Airfield

BUILDING REPLICA AIRCRAFT

Before he came to Cornwall, Viv had been involved in building replica aircraft, some of which were used in films, including "The Battle of Britain". Viv Bellamy flew in that Production. He was the driving force: he knew what he wanted and would call all the shots. This resulted in the construction of several `one-off` replica aircraft: Sopwith Camel, Sopwith one & half strutter, a DH2, a Fokker DRIG-BEFR tri-plane – the first replica to be made, Fairey Flycatcher, Mackie seaplane, S 5 replica and the world`s only example of a Fairey Albacore N4172.

This took four years to construct arriving at Yeovilton on the 16th April 1987 for exhibition at the Fleet Air Arm museum minus its wings, which were made elsewhere. A wooden Supermarine S5 was also constructed but subsequently crashed at Pencarrow Point, Mylor on the 28th May 1987 killing Mr. Bill Hosie its then owner.

Rod recalls a Messcheschmit being at the Airfield, and it disappearing. One day the Owner just came in, and took it away. There was very limited hangarage. By the time they got a Rapide and a Cessna in the hangar there was very little room for an Engineer! The Rapide had to basically go in sideways. `About thirty shuffles to get it out in the summer` quipped Jeff Bold. There was still a lot of interest in aviation at this time. People came just watch the aircraft, both in flight and under construction.

One special plane made at St. Just Airport was *`The Fury`, designed and built by John Isaacs, with assistance from Bill Penaluna, Jeff Bold, with Sue Marshall rib-stitching the fabric on the wings with Waxed string. In a small room in the Clubhouse fronting the road, Eric Watson had the unenviable task of coating the wings with thirteen coats of `dope`.

He remembered the stink being so bad that he had to sit out in the air for a while before he could drive home. The engine for this aircraft came from a museum in New Zealand. Dave Ring flew the Fury, and worked in the Café.

A Bird's Eye View

Viv Bellamy had been involved with construction and flying those types of planes for some time and they were all built in the original hangar with the workshop in the middle and in what is now, the Freight Shed.

The buildings on site had not really changed much. The water tower was converted into the Control tower many years later the works carried out by Penwith District Council. Alan Hunt lifted the Air Traffic Control Box onto the Tower with his crane. If you had visited the site about seventy years ago, it would have almost looked the same. Still grass runways. New hangars now, and a bit more 'hard-standing'. But changes were on their way!

Gull's eye views

By August, Coastal Flights from Land`s End [St. Just] Aerodrome were offered by Westward Airways [Land`s End] Ltd as 'an aerial tour of West Penwith in modern nine-seater Britten Norman Islander Aircraft. Gull's eye views at only 3 pound per seat or 25 pound party rate, also, local coastal flights-reduced rates on first full morning flight booked ate aerodrome. Other tours, Charters arranged`. `Why not visit Islander food bar and lounge – now open to the general public – no obligation to fly-courtesy-quality-value-excellent grandstand view of Airfield`

31

Lands End Airfield
1971

August saw the formation of Vivian H Bellamy's Westward Airways (Land's End). It applied for a route to St. Mary's using Brymon's Islander, GAXXJ, but no services were actually flown. The most romantic aircraft the above operated was the Dragon Rapide G-A1YR. Westward Airways operated as a Training School for over twenty years and had taught P.P.L, I.M.C. and R.T.L. Also offered were conversions from `tricycle-to-tail dragger, helicopter to fixed-wing and micro-light-to-light aircraft`. `It was very much a father-and-son enterprise, with son Roderick Bellamy as Chief Engineer and a craftsman of repute` said Hugh Scanlan, Rod having rebuilt and repainted a Dragon Rapide.

John Baker of C.A.A. (Civil Aviation Authority) recalls in the early seventies, in Viv Bellamy's time, "the airport was a fascinating place for a young man intent on learning to fly. In the workshops, a replica vintage aircraft always seemed to be under construction and the airfield was home to a DH Rapide and a privately owned Percival Prentice that was a rather ungainly machine, and this example had seen better days. It sat outside in all weathers."

To John's untrained eye, it didn't look very airworthy. But the owner would fly regularly, arriving in great haste to start-up the engine and roar off towards St. Mawgan, to return a few hours later. Apparently, his navigation technique involved following the coastline at low level about a mile out to sea. John, personally never saw the Prentice fly, but at each visit, eagerly hoped to witness the event, because it was reckoned to be an exciting affair. It seemed that the Prentice owner's wife didn't approve of her husband's flying activities. Frequently, shortly after he had reached the Aerodrome, she would arrive in a taxi to try and prevent his departure. The story has it, that on one occasion, she arrived in time to be able to climb up on the wing to remonstrate with him. With great presence of mind, he opened the throttle, and the Slipstream blew her off the wing. Free once more, he taxied out and took off.

There was an Airtourer at Lands End, which John flew in a couple of times with an Instructor from the Culdrose Gliding Club who told John that this Aircraft, which had an unusual single `spade` control column between the pilots, flew like a Spitfire. Being so over-awed with this idea, it never occurred to him to ask how he knew this. In those frugal days, any flying was welcome. So John cleaned a very smart Retractable single` [but doesn't recall what it was], in the hope that the local Doctor who owned it would give him a trip. The late John Boyns of Levant also had a share in a plane. Ronnie Jelbert - plane and a Pilot and flew to France regularly on Business.

Island Air Charter G-AYCV, June 1971

A Bird's Eye View

Ian Harding of Bristol, a configuration engineer with Airbus UK Filton, Bristol has a life-long interest in aviation and has worked with British Aerospace for over 32 years. A member of PFA (popular Flying Association) for 10 years, his Father worked for BEA/British Airways for 33 years, starting at Whitchurch, Bristol. He had previously been with Olley Air Services. Ian first flew from Land`s End Aerodrome in 1960 in a DH89A Rapide to St. Mary's, Isles of Scilly. He had also flown to the Islands by air in 1970/71 in the S-61 helicopter.

1972

In January, Westward Airways acquired DH89A Dragon Rapide, G-AIYR. This was used by Land's End Aero Club. The aircraft was employed for pleasure flying and parachute dropping and was the last of its type to fly commercially in the UK (eventually withdrawn in 1978 and is now at Duxford museum). Other aircraft used by Westward Airways were Cessna's 150, 152, 172, FR172, a Super Skymaster (G-BCBZ), an Apache (G-ASEP), a Cherokee (G-ASPK), an Autocrat (G-AHAP) a Devon (G-BLPZ) and various others.

On June 9th, a two-seater Airtourer light aeroplane: G-AYMF, on lease from Glos. Air Ltd, crashed after over-shoot soon after take-off from Land`s End Airport. Ken Wood, then a young Constable, was first on the scene, along with Roger Jenkin of Higher Tregiffian Farm, recalled `one of the fliers already appeared to be dead, the other had his seat-belt unfastened`. The pilot Keith Waterfield, a former Income Tax Inspector, suffered a fractured skull was eventually taken to Plymouth General Hospital. He eventually recovered from his injuries. The passenger Edward Ushaw, a watch-maker, married with a baby, sadly died. It was reported that an inaccurate fuel gauge may have contributed to the aircraft running out of fuel. It was climbing away from the airfield after a missed approach when the engine stopped.

In June Captain John Nurse first flew into Land's End Aerodrome in 1966 and had seen huge changes there "not always for the better". He recalls the Café being built by Mike Reynolds and Gabeh Monroe. Gabe was also the photographer for Brian Neeley. Mike Reynolds used raffia table mats to decorate the cement counter, and, the walls. The roof always leaked.

John first worked as a Flying Instructor in June 1972 and must have done 3 or 4 tours of duty instructing. The Flying Club was a fun place and one of the few things that Viv Bellamy and John Nurse agreed: "That flying should always be fun. When people who were spending a lot of money and paying our wages, no matter how good or bad they were, deserved to enjoy their flying". Most of the fondest memories of John's life came from those days.

1975

Now having a Flying Club at Land's End Airport in the mid-1970's,, it was listed in the "Flight International" magazine, in the, "Where to Fly" South & South-West section.

Lands End Airfield

Courses included: PPL, IMC, Twin and Aerobatics. The Fleet consisted of: 1 Glos Airtourer (£15), 1 Cessna 172 (£15) and 1 Apache 235 (£50). Membership Fees were: £7.50 (Full) and £1 (Temp).

1977
Freddy Stribley, [`aka` D.J. Freddy Zapp and once an Official Monster Raving Looney Candidate]], on leaving school took up an apprenticeship as a panel beater and sprayer in Redruth. Later running his own business and acknowledged as one of the best in Cornwall in the trade. Such was his reputation that he was `hired` to re-spray a World War One Fokker tri-plane, identical to that flown by the Red Barron built at St. Just Airfield. It was one of his proudest moments when he watched it take part in an aerobatics display.

1979
The short lived Eastern Green Airlines emerged. This was an air taxi concern using Seneca GBASM.

1981
Skybus with connections to the Isles of Scilly Steamship Co. operated from Land`s End to St. Mary's carrying freight etc. as well as passengers using Islander aircraft along with de Havilland DHC6 Twin Otter on longer routes.
Westward Airways again put forward plans for a service to St. Mary's but British Airways Helicopters (BAH) in Penzance (successors from BEA Helicopters) objected and this was upheld.

1983
The Scillies became national news following a crash on the 16th July. BAH S-61N helicopter, G-BEON, crashed in poor visibility 2 miles out from St. Mary's. Of the 26 people on board only 6 survived.

1984
Early in 1984 the Isles of Scilly Steamship Company formed a subsidiary to operate to the Islands from St. Just, to offer both transport by sea and air. The new service to the Isles of Scilly from Lands End was operated with Britten-Norman nine-seater aircraft and the first aircraft owned by the Company was Islander G-BFNU. The first Pilots were Captain John Nurse and the Manager of the Airport, Captain Vivian Bellamy.

A Bird's Eye View

*Up to 9 persons, plus baggage £115 up 5 persons, plus baggage £90
Prices quoted are one-way, and include VAT. Departure times: "Flexible to suit your needs, when possible. Normally on the Hour – and, Half Hour from St Marys.
Don't delay - book today!*

A new player emerged in the spring. The Isles of Scilly Steamship Company (ISSC) applied to operate a scheduled daily passenger and freight aircraft service between Land's End and St. Mary's, proposing to use a Skyvan. The intention was to provide a service complimentary to that of the ship Scillonian (also owned by ISSC). Not surprisingly British Airways Helicopters objected stating there was insufficient demand to sustain two services.

July – The ISSC's proposed airline, Skybus, had its application rejected.

Aug – Not withstanding the refused application, the ISSC purchased Islander, G-BNFU, for charter work. The aircraft made its first trip from Land's End to St. Mary's on the 9th of August.

Winter – Two further Islanders were used by Skybus (G-BJWL and G-BCEN) which were used to fly early flowers from St. Mary's

1985

One Thursday in January 1985 Peter Channon at the grand age of 35, started out on a big adventure, leaving behind his wife Pam and baby son Mark, flying his tiny Comper Swift single engine plane from St. Just Airfield, to Biggin Hill, hoping to recreate the epic 12,000 mile flight, from Britain to Australia made by an Australian aviator around 50 years previously. Unfortunately Peter never completed the project but he did make a start.

IMAGE: Mike Hicks, Chairman Isles of Scilly Council 2012 has had a long standing involvement with the airfield.

35

Lands End Airfield

In the spring the Council of the Isles of Scilly looked at establishing a new fixed-wing site on the mainland. As far back as 1972 a site at Leedstown was considered as was using the facilities at Culdrose and exploratory talks were held about expanding the Penzance heliport. None of these came about.

LURE OF THE ISLES FOR THE PEARMANS

Peter and Stephanie Jane Pearman `ran away` to get married and had their married blessed in the Old Town Church, St. Mary's, Isle of Scilly. They decided that it would be wonderful place to have their 3 month old daughter christened. As St. Buryan was `in-between` Vicars they were given permission. The Reverend Peter Woodall was pleased to christen their daughter since he had blessed the couple the previous year.

A plane was booked to carry the family: Parents, baby, Grandparents, God-parents and two children, from St. Just to St. Mary's on a Saturday in September 1985, and to return later in the afternoon. The `weather` had been glorious up until that very Saturday…the fog came down and it was `no-go`!

A friend, who was also to be Godmother, was enjoying her holiday on St. Mary's and had made up a table of party food, collecting the `fishing-boat` shape christening cake, in readiness for the `Do`. This now had to go in the fridge until the group could get there. Sunday of course, was lovely gain, which was of no use since no planes were able to fly commercially. Monday dawned misty again, with their hopes of ever getting across fading, the telephone rang at 10.30 a.m. with the message `now or never` - so it was `now` [after ringing the Vicar and settling the dog!]

Everyone was scooped up and they had an exciting flight over, a perfect service [with the baby crying throughout] followed by a good old sing-song at the house- then the mist once again descended! Thank goodness for the friend who stayed in such a large house on the Battery. After `champagne `n chips` they all managed to find a corner – three –in-bed- and `newly christened ~Tabitha Rosemary Rainbow` in a drawer!

The next day, still in their best `bib and tucker` and Tabitha in her gown, they returned home safely, very glad and privileged that, at last, Tabitha had been christened in that magical church. Many thanks were given to Mike Vigar who was very helpful over the booking.

A Bird's Eye View

THE PERFECT LADY

A television documentary entitled 'The Perfect Lady' began filming at the airfield. on 22nd July 1985. The subject being the two seater Spitfire T9ML407, formerly of the Irish Air Corps owned by Nick and Caroline Grace, who later moved to a new home at Middle Wallop.

In September British Airways sold its helicopter subsidiary at Penzance and it was renamed British International Helicopters (BIH). In December, Skybus added another Islander, GSBUS to its fleet.

1987

A restricted passenger licence was finally granted to Skybus to operate a scheduled service between Land's End and St. Mary's. Later that year these restrictions were eased. Skybus was successful in its application to the C.A.A. for a passenger air Route licence in February 1987. Barnsleslie Ward, the Chairman of the parent company was 'absolutely delighted' and a happy company executive Chairman, Mr. Charles Cartwright, thought that there was a lot of potential in day trips for Islanders and visitors alike. Pilots for the aircraft were Captain Mike Boyle, a former Concorde pilot, and Captain John Nurse, who learnt to fly with the Kent 'Tiger Club'. Brymon Airways sent a letter congratulating the Company on their route licensing award and welcomed them to the ranks of international air transport. They also looked forward to a close and growing association over the years. B.I.H and its predecessor, British Airways [later in private ownership], the Islands Council and Cornwall County Council had been amongst objectors to the application.

Skybus original scheme was to run a Short Skyvan. But failure at the initial licence attempt forced it to adapt. It kept faith with the Islander aircraft, adding a second and had been operating a successful freight run. It also dropped the number of movements sought.

D. H. Dragon and D.H. Dragon Rapide visited Land's End on 14th September 1987, en route to St. Mary's, Isles of Scilly, for the 50th anniversary of scheduled Services to the Isles of Scilly. The late Hugh Scanlan once recalled his flight in a BEA de Havilland Dragon Rapide from Land's End to the Scilly Isles "as fun, this was flying!" (Courtesy Aeroplane Monthly, Oct. 1987)

During July and August a Microlight Round Britain Rally visited the field. It flew in from Aylesbury, Bucks, then to Lands End, landing 1 p.m. approx. and then on to Barton, Manchester.

Lands End Airfield

1988

An Air day was held on 25th August 1988. Early visitors to the field included Harry Seacombe and Richard Branson. The Monster Raving Looney Party also visited the airfield.

38

A Bird's Eye View

1989
A new hanger was erected (now housing the engineering facilities) and the tower was refurbished. A proposal to tarmac the runways was abandoned. By now Islanders, G-PASZ, G-BESO, G-AXWP and G-AXWR were all used by Skybus.

1990 AIR TRAINING CORPS
Each year a contract was offered to various airfields around the UK - including Lands End - to train Air Training Corps pilots for the RAF. In order to teach the Cadets, the Company wrote to the Ministry and received approval. It was still fairly easy at that time. Under the management of Rod Bellamy, this was a great success at the field, with the students billeted at his house right alongside the field. The students flew during the day and read their manuals during the evenings - so we were told!

COLIN SHAW
Pilot Instructor Colin Shaw was a key figure at the Flying School for many years. With a strong RAF background, he proved to be a great pilot instructor, requiring accurate flying from his students at all times. He was also in love with aerobatics and was often in the Cessna 152 Aerobat looping and diving over Pendeen lighthouse, the favoured area. He signed off many local pilots, including numerous ATC students that were posted at Lands End for the purpose.

It was a very unfortunate affair in 1990s when Colin offered to undertake the test flying of the new Skybolt. Both he and the new owner went off on a the first flight, but following aerobatics over Penzance Bay they lost control and both were killed. Everyone from the Airfield and Club turned out for the very moving funeral.

Mike Durand who was to marry Helen Mansfield, the Secretary/Manager of the Flying Club, was a popular flying instructor for many years. Danielle Pitman recalled that Mike would always direct taxiing with great accuracy "Don't go there, turn left now ..." She found out later that Mike used to pick mushrooms off the airfield for his tea. Mike lived in a caravan parked at the North Eastern end of the buildings. One night thieves broke into the Clubhouse, but first wedged his caravan door closed with a pole. At daylight, when all was clear he climbed out the window and raised the alarm.

Lands End Airfield

1991 REGULAR VISITORS

Dave Gillard said that it was with great relief that he first saw Lands End Airfield, when in October 1991, he was sent on his first cross-country solo flight from Bodmin Airfield, as part of his training for his pilots licence. He was not aware at that time that Lands End Aerodrome would become such a favourite for an away landing! David said that he has always received a warm welcome, enjoyed good conversation and received good advice from Members of the Flying Club including Mr. John Boyns of Levant, and the `Folks` in the Tower. Many a walk from the airfield to the Coastal cliff path had been followed by a visit to the Choxaway Cafe, and another warm welcome from Rose and Ron who managed it so successfully.

David said `I can thoroughly recommend the food, particularly the coffee cake and Cornish Clotted cream to round it all off, what a better way to complete the day, than to enjoy a flight back along the North coast to Bodmin!"

Kathy and Colin Knowles from Exeter have been flying to the Scillies for last eight years. One of their lasting impressions of Land`s End Aerodrome, was their very first flight. They didn't know what to expect as they had only flown from large airports before. When they arrived and parked, they managed to enter by the back door! So they climbed over the weighing-scales with their suitcases. Kathy was highly amused at being weighed with her hand luggage. But she thinks that her outstanding memory of that very first flight from Lands End was her amusement at the announcement "would the Whites, Browns and the Smiths assemble by the patio doors." That was the point when Kathy and Colin both burst out laughing. It epitomizes the small, friendly lovely approach to passengers at Land`s End Aerodrome

Jonathan Chappell and Mike Boyd first flew into Land`s End for the 1999 Eclipse and camped under the wing of their aircraft Yak 52 LY-AFA, usually based at Barton, Manchester. Their second visit was to re-fuel after a trip to the Isles of Scilly on 17th August 2001. They liked the airfield, "but thought it a challenge to find the right runway! The Choxaway Cafe` seemed an excellent place to re-fuel the `inner-man`.

Image: one of the many evening "do's" at the Flying Club

A Bird's Eye View

1992
A new long term lease for the aerodrome was agreed between the council Joint Committee and Westward Airways (Land's End) Ltd. In May, Islander, GSSKY was purchased by Skybus.

1993
On Friday 9th July about 30 Fournier powered gliders arrived from Germany, Belgium, France, Holland, and Switzerland. Because of fog, they stayed camped on the field longer than they intended, but a great time was had by all. Lots of `Entente Cordiale`. Brian Porch, a founder Club member was at his usual post - the BBQ. John Boyns, one of the elders of the Club with years of war experience was approached by several of the German flyers, who asked if he has ever visited Germany. "Only for deliveries" was his reply.

Islander G-AXWP
Since the I.O.S. Skybus Company decided to introduce a Twin Otter to its routes some of the Islander aircraft were put up for sale. Islander G-AXWP was sold to Montserrat Airways that operates from Montserrat, one of the Leward Island group in the Caribbean. Captain David Leatherdale, together with their pilot, Peter Morris flew it there.

Peter collected WP from LEA and flew it to Guernsey where Aurigny Airlines fitted a ferry tank system and re-sprayed the plane Montserrat Airlines colours – involving re-spraying the white and over-spraying the Skybus blue & red striping with green & yellow stripe and changing the airline name on the forward fuselage. It was registered before the trip, the new reg. of VP-LMH which was also painted on. VP is the designation for British overseas dependencies; L specifies the Leeward Islands and M Montserrat. H is unique to the aircraft as it's an unusual registration controllers on route asked where it was from & bound.

The ferry tanks consisted of three 45 Imperial gallon drums mounted across the fuselage on a pair of shaped wooden beams and lashed to the floor with cables. Seats were removed and stowed in the luggage locker as the tanks covered most of the floor. Therefore paneling was removed from the centre fuselage and rubber hoses carrying the fuel from the drums were plumbed into the aircraft fuel system between the normal fuel cocks and the engines. A control panel, could be reached by twisting round in the pilot's seat, was lashed to the front drum, about a foot behind the seats. Mounted on this were a fuel cock for each engine and switches for the electric fuel pumps of which there were two for each engine. On the side of each drum, now on top, was a screw in filler cap with a vent tube in the centre connected by hoses to the aircraft fuel venting system. When refueling, these hoses had to be removed from the caps before the caps themselves could be unscrewed, Aurigny made some aluminum spanners to fit the connectors and caps. So, there was not much room for luggage, so we they had to lie things on top of the tanks which had to be removes when filling. Refueling was, therefore, a fairly involved business! As they found, most refuellers were not permitted to pump fuel into fuselage tanks, so that had to do it themselves.

Lands End Airfield

After several hiccups the intrepid pair flew to their final destination via Stanstead to Glasgow, flying at 10,000 feet just above the cloud tops picking up a little ice; Faroe Islands; Reykjavik Iceland; Greenland; Iqaluit Canada, Newport News, Fort Lauderdale Executive Airport, Grand Turk Caicos Isles and finally Montserrat.

It had been seven days since David and Peter had left Stanstead, during which time they covered 6,100 nautical miles and logged nearly 47 hours flying time. Without delays due to weather and the difficulty in obtaining U.S. charts it would have taken five days. David said he didn't think the prospect of strong winds increasing flight times between St. Mary's and Exeter from 1 hour to 1 ¼ would seem quite so daunting!

1993 was also a memorable year for David and Danielle Pitman, members of the Lands End Aero Club who successfully passed their PPL exams, went on to purchase their own plane and became regular visitors to the field. Many other members were completing exams and training around this time.

Rod Bellamy was the driving force at the airfield at this time. He was both MD and Chief Engineer for Westawrd Airways and also one of the best GA instructors in the UK.. The airfield was personalised by his collection of classic cars and the numerous interesting aeroplanes that came and went under his control. After flying some would "jump in the old Rolls and go up the chip shop".

The airfield has a Riems Cessna G-AWWU for Scenic Flights. On clear summer days this attraction was most popular with passing holiday makers. So much so that Rod employed a full time pilot and "stuffer". On a busy day, the pilot rarely got out and the stuffer's job was to bring the next 'victims' to the plane and 'stuff them in'.

On one special summers day the Scenic Flights had more than 100 'victims' enjoy a flight over the scenic South West peninsular.

Images: Danielle & David Pitman,
Rod Bellamy and Rose after a scenic trip,
Mike Vigar with Jill Thomas winner of the European Championships 1993

42

A Bird's Eye View

Image De Haviland Dragon DH89 [G-ACZE] visiting Land's End Aerodrome, May 1993

Image Rt: Trevor, John Boyns, & Frank Fish take a ride on the airfield.

1994

The ISSC purchased its first Twin Otter aircraft n April, GBIHO, to operate its 'up-country' routes from Newquay, Exeter, Bristol and Southampton. This aircraft was ex-Brymon but purchased from Abu Dhabi.

Throughout this period there were many social parties and gatherings in and around the Club, leading to all sorts of trouble and headaches. Ringleaders were often Rod Bellamy and Frank (the Fish) Knowles, Captain of a deep sea trawler from Newlyn.

On returning to Port, Frank would make his first visit the flying club. Some time, and many gins later his 'bird' would hear that he was ashore and come looking for him.

1995

Feb – Islander, GBUBN was purchased by Skybus. It was also around this time that the 'white house' at the end of runway 18 was sold to an owner from outside the area. He quickly started a campaign against the airfield although flying had been operational since 1937. A consistent flow of complaints were received and duly noted - until one day it was noticed that the wind had changed and the planes were using a completely different runway pattern. It then became apparent that the calls were being managed.

43

Lands End Airfield

Image: Pilots Danielle Pitman, Frank the Fish and Rod Bellamy at Rods house at the end of the runway.

Image: Standing in front of a visiting 1943 AT6 Harvard, Members of the Hayle Camera Club on a `Field Trip` to L.E.A. 22nd July 1995 (Courtesy Colin Rew)

1996

In 1996 Frank 'the Fish' Knowles, Captain of one of the larger Newlyn trawlers, signed up with Bill Penaluna to become part of a three person syndicate to build and own a Skybolt. When this was announced, it caused great discussion at the field, as Bill was a big bloke and a quick calculation would confirm that the biplane would not be capable of carrying both Bill and Frank. So Frank would have to fly mono. Shortly after a sheet of paper went up on the board, selling grandstand tickets along the 35 runway to watch the inaugural flight.

1997

In July 1997, the management at Land`s End Aerodrome notified the CAA of plans to provide a paved runway. Plans to improve aeronautical ground lighting [runway lighting] and an approach slope indicator system, which is required for scheduled public transport operations at any time. The runway and lighting plans subsequently ran into planning problems and were eventually abandoned; however, the requirements to provide a minimum approach slope indicator system, known as and an Abbreviated Precision Approach Path Indicator [APAPI] system remained.

A Precision Approach Path Indicator [PAPI] system consists of four light units located adjacent to the runway [usually to the left of the approach] at the point where touchdown would be expected. The four light units provide a visual signal, in a combination of white and red lights, to pilots on approach to indicate the correct approach path angle. A combination of four white lights or three white and one red light, indicates that the aircraft is too high; four red lights or three red and one white indicates too low; and two white and two red indicates the correct approach angle. An APAPI system consists of just two light units to provide a three-stage indication of high, low and on-slope guidance. The correct approach angle is essential to provide adequate clearance from obstacles on the approach.

Despite considerable opposition to the planning application to install the APAPI system on runway 35, planning permission was eventually obtained.

A Bird's Eye View

2000

Over the August Bank Holiday weekend Jean and Warren Chmura of Cot Valley gave Charity helicopter rides raising over fifteen hundred pounds! It was a bit manic at times but very exciting and was immensely enjoyed by all at the airfield.

CHAOTIC COOKBOOK

The "Chaotic Cookbook" was launched, penned by Rose and Lesley from the Chox's Away Cafe – with recipes tried & tested by Pilots and friends - in support of the `Mermaid Centre` at RCH Treliske. Lesley Double and Sandra Matthews, famed for her `rock buns`, were members of Choxaway Cafe `Team` at the airport.

Lands End suffers from really strong winds and on this occasion the Trinity House portacabin was blown over by the gales.

Toyah Wilcox also visited the field prior to a flight with Trinity to Godrevy Lighthouse in April 2000.

45

Lands End Airfield

TRINITY HOUSE

An air service operated from Penwith and Scilly during the latter years of the Twentieth Century that should not be overlooked were Bond Helicopters – working under contract to Trinity House.

They were employed taking keepers to-and-fro off-shore lighthouses after helipads were installed above their lanterns during the 1970s and early 1980s and before they were all automated. Off the Penwith coast these were namely: The Longships, The Wolf Rock, The Bishop Rock and Round Island.

Exchange of Crews to the Seven Stones Lightship was also carried out after a helipad was fitted. These helicopters have also been used to carry out maintenance duties since automation. At least some of these duties were carried out from a pad at Sennen. These duties were much speedier than earlier days with the Trinity House Tenders, such as `Satellite` and `Stella1 hindered by heavy weather. Trinity House originally built the dwellings in Marias Lane, Sennen to house the keepers from Longships Lighthouse whilst they were ashore [and their families]. The relief of the duty keepers on the Lighthouse was carried out by sea.

In the early 1970s the helicopter began to be used for the relief, an operating area for the aircraft was constructed in the grounds of the dwellings.

With the automation of the lighthouse in the western rocks [Bishop Rock, Round Island, Wolf Rock and Longships] the keepers were posted to other stations that were still manned. The dwellings were vacated and eventually sold in 1988. At this time the Trinity House helicopter operation for the western rocks was moved to Land`s End Airport where it is today.

Image: Visiting Cadets from 147 Squadron [Camborne] Air Training C Mick Yould, Deputy Hangar Foreman [Westward Airways] at St. Just Airfield.

A Bird's Eye View

Skybus Staff 'Check-in Desk' version of the 'Full Monty' June 1998. Left to right: Chris Spence [Rampy], Mike Vigar, [Traffic Manager], Phil Harvey [Rampy], Mike Smith [Fireman], Paul Williams [Ops. Manager] and Mike Stevens [Fireman]

The Skybus Team at Lands End Aeroport

Skybus Pilots included:

Richard Ashby
Rob Atherton
Warwick Bayman
Frank Bentley
Steve Bird
Chris Bryning
Simon Burke
Peter Channon
Lottie Chittenden
Martin Dowling
Adrian Eves
John Foster
Jack Hawkins
John Holmes
Patrick Keen
David Leatherdale
John Nurse
Brian O'Driscoll
Nigel Perkins
Chris Price
Martin Shrewsbury
Brian Sperring
Richard Songer
Toby Songer
Guy Walters
Rob Willis
Mike Hicks, Chairman of ISSSC/Skybus in July 1999

47

Lands End Airfield
2001 CLOSED BID AUCTION
The Council Joint Committee who owned the aerodrome decided to sell the freehold in a closed bid auction. A property company in London, Ambercroft Properties Ltd., submitted the highest bid and purchased the aerodrome for £376,000. The ISSC continued as the aerodromes tenants.

THREE SURVIVE PLANE CRASH
On Sunday 6th May 2001 at approximately 3.15 p.m. a visiting Tobago Aircraft flown by Sir Richard Noble of Farnborough, holder of the land-speed record, got into difficulties as it tried to land at Lands End Aerodrome. The three people on board were very fortunate to walk away unscathed, and, were well enough to travel home by train. The Tobago was seriously damaged.

This emphasizes the difficulties of some approaches to coastal airfields, where sloping ground or cliffs on the approach can cause serious downwinds or turbulence. Those without local experience can suddenly find themselves landing earlier than they expected.

Thursday 13th September 2001
New Notice in Skybus Departure Lounge:
"Resulting from the atrocious acts of terrorism in the U.S.A. on Wednesday 11th September SKYBUS at Lands End have put the following procedures into practice:

The D.E.T.R. requires passengers and their baggage to be searched prior to boarding flights. We apologize for any inconvenience, or, delay which may result. LUGGAGE MUST NOT BE LEFT UNATTENDED. Passengers refusing to co-operate will be denied boarding. We thank you for your understanding and assistance".

2002 APAPI LANDING SYSTEM
Despite the considerable local opposition to the planning application to install the APAPI system on runway 35, planning permission was granted in 2002 and a team of engineers from nearby Culdrose duly installed the APAPI units. They were set-up to give the standard on-slope angle of 3 degrees with a mean eye height above threshold [MEHT] of 8m. The MEHT represents the design height of the pilot's eyes when the aircraft crosses the runway threshold and is used to assure the obstacle clearance requirements are met and to calculate the installation location of the units.

On 19th October 2002, a commissioning check of the APAPI units on runway 35 was conducted by the CAA; however the commissioning flight check was abandoned when it was realized that the visual signals were indicating at least 200 feet lower than expected. The installation criteria and calculations were rechecked and it was decided by the CAA that an increase in the approach angle to 4 degrees would be acceptable without the need to relocate the APAPI units.

On 5th November 2002, the CAA revisited the aerodrome and the APAPI units were realigned for a 4-degree approach slope. The weather conditions [visibility less 100m in drizzle] made flying impossible at the time. However a later flight check reported satisfactory visual guidance and the APAPI system was declared operational.

SECOND TWIN OTTER ADDED

In June the ISSC added a second Twin Otter to its fleet, G-CBML. The aircraft was ferried across from North America by the Skybus Chief Pilot, Captain Richard Ashby.

Peter Channon was a regular at Lands End, firstly as a long time Skybus pilot and additionally as a private pilot in the area. Brian Sperrng and Peter Channon also purchased Perranporth Airfield, just along the coast Later, Peter was also known for his banner towing from the field and his aerial photography around Cornwall.

John Holmes, one of the Commercial Pilots lived with his wife June (involved with Twinning with French Town) at Wadebridge. With a great sense of humour, he once walked out into the passenger lounge wearing dark glasses and tapping a white stick...calling for the passengers to follow him to plane!

Lands End Airfield

Andrew Evans, pictured here with Dave Rowe in March 2002, was the youngest member of Land`s End Flying Club. He had been interested in flying and aircraft since the age of seven. His first experience of flight and aircraft was at Culdrose International Air day, so much enjoyed for he could see the pilots stepping out of their aircraft and everyone applauding at the sight of a man or woman that had just performed a series of aerobatics to impress the crowds. His tenth birthday present was a trial flying lesson at Land`s End. Andrew was so excited because the family used to fly from LEA to the Scillies, in Islander aircraft, for their holidays. The flying lesson went very well, the Instructor, with his Dad also on board, flew over Andrew's home at 13,00 feet – he could see absolutely everything, even the small vegetable patch!.

In October, 2001, he had joined the aero club as a social member – he got to know the pilots and the aircraft. Now 13, he was counting the days to his 14 birthday when he could start flight training. His ambition? To be an instructor for a large company in flight training!

The Austin Seven Club made several `trips` to LEA, one such from Hayle to Land`s End Airport on 18 May 2002 when twenty cars took part: including 1930 `Rubies, Boxes and Chummy`s`. These cars always created much interest, as did the motor-bikes on Sunday rides. The Club's `route` sheet also contained a local quiz and. After `refreshing` stay, the option to venture to Porthgwarra – a small cove with tunnel cut in the rock by St. Just miners years ago, to make landing of caught fish easier.

50

A Bird's Eye View

SCENIC FLIGHTS ... A Pilot's Account
Related by Mawgan Grace - January 2002.

To the west, on the horizon lie the Isles of Scilly, an enchanted group of islands with their bright golden beaches glistening enticingly over thirty miles away. Below me, the water is turquoise. Surfers in their coloured wet suits are the only reminder that the water is not as warm and tropical as sometimes imagined! Straight ahead, now we are facing Cape Cornwall and the miniature toy towns of St. Just and Pendeen in the distance. Scanning the horizon for possible airborne Traffic as we approach the Aerodrome, it is impossible not to stare in awe. I can see the St. Austell Alps to the east, and the most. Southerly point of Britain, the Lizard to the further south. It seems as if I am at the end of the World.

Instinctively woken up from the tranquil bliss, I realize sadly our journey must soon come to an end, and, it is time to come down. On a day like today, I begrudgingly complete my pre-descent checks and turn to make sure that my Passengers are still happy and secure. My Passengers. In the last few moments, I had selfishly believed that my experience was personal, and now realize that I must again share my gift with these less fortunate ground living mortals.

Slipping over Sennen Cove I gently close the throttle fully, and aim for the south of the Aerodrome, for today we are required by physics, to land northerly on runway 35. The noisy reliable sound of the powerful engine has softened, and we can enjoy a natural approach to the runway. I'm expecting my passengers to respond quizzically

51

Lands End Airfield

to this now quieter form of flight. On previous occasions passengers would ask, "What would happen if the noise were to stop"?

In an attempt to put the world to rights, I therefore mention that we are indeed gliding, and, that the `worst case scenario` is indeed quite safe and pleasurable. Not only should the Aerodrome neighbours agree with me, from a noise aspect, but also if the engine were to stop for any reason away from the Aerodrome, I would personally feel comfortable in putting her down in an adequate field. As we circle in, on approach, my sight catches the windsock. This relic from the first days of aviation has remained almost unchanged. It represents a faithful friend to all pilots, with its completely honest simple design still essential at the world's most modern airports. As we whistle over the impassive cows on short final, the Runway is soon streaking beneath us. A gentle flare precedes the familiar rumble of the undercarriage on the daisy-strewn runway. Rabbits stop and stare momentarily as we pass by. The dream is over.

Applying power to taxi back to the Clubhouse, the passengers erupt with pleasure. Any anxiety there might have been from their unfamiliar world, transforms into unconfined emotion. Stopping out the 1930s Clubhouse, Family members, that watched us from the ground madly wave and smile.

With a pull of the mixture control, I shut off the petrol supply, starving the fuel Injected six cylinders, and the burbling engine runs down. After switching-off the electric, the only sound remaining are the gyros winding down over the Hot ticking noise from the exhaust. Passengers excitedly burst out of the Aircraft in their rapture, quoting stories of a miniature world, with caves, Lighthouses and matchstick people in a childish zeal.

As I say goodbye to my latest acquaintances, I wonder if they realize that I have just introduced them to a very personal and sacred world up there with the clouds. I do believe though, that it is an experience they are not likely to forget Relaxing with a cup of tea, I look out of the window across the Aerodrome to the ocean. The sky still beckons, and I keenly await my next visitors, so that we may again embark on another special journey in the majesty of flight over West Cornwall.

A Bird's Eye View

2003 RAF RE-UNION

In October 2003, 75 year old Bernard Maslin from Chippenham in Wiltshire, (an ex Traffic Controller who served on 4 aircraft carriers and a submarine depot ship; former Antiques Dealer, who gained his PPL in 1979 at Biggin Hill, followed up with IMC and night ratings, now with 2,500 flying hours under his belt) was heading, along with his friends to a Fleet Air Arm Squadron Reunion at the Isles of Scilly.

Bernard, Dennis and Arthur, with combined ages 239 years had taken-off from St. Just Lands End Aerodrome and miraculously survived a ditching in fixed-gear high wing Cessna 172. The weather was slightly hazy, with a brisk headwind for the 12 minute flight to St. Mary's, Scilly. Wearing lifejackets for their trip over the sea, Dennis was in the right seat, Arthur in the back, Bernard piloting. Out of the group of assembled nine aircraft heading for the reunion, they were 7th to leave. When they were at 2,000 feet, seven miles from Scillies the engine cut out because of a fuel problem. Bernard ran through the restart procedure.

Dennis helped by switching tanks but all to no avail, the aircraft was dying. Bernard spotted a boat and tried to get near to it. A Mayday call to Scillies was made. The plane was down to 900 feet in less than two minutes. The crew opened doors and windows then looked for a crest of wave on which to land. Bernard kept pulling back on the controls and the plane seemed almost vertical when the tail touched the water, the aircraft settled initially with the cabin under water. The people aboard the fishing vessel saw the happenings, hauling in their fishing nets before they could get to the Pilots.

40 minutes after ditching Bernard was hauled aboard the fishing vessel "Semper Allegro" where his two friends sat with their hands wrapped around steaming mugs of tea!
A "Sea King" on exercise in the vicinity, took Bernard to the Royal Cornwall Hospital, Treliske, where he recovered from "near drowning". The amount of seawater he had consumed actually increased his weight by 50 per cent! Arthur suffered a nasty injury that took off some of his finger nails, caused when his hand became trapped between the horizontal stabilizer and elevator after he clung onto the tail. Arthur asked the nurses to wrap them in big bandages so that it would look like he'd been in the Wars! The Trio's Tales will be told at many a Reunion Dinner now!

Lands End Airfield

2004
Skybus celebrated its 20th Anniversary on the 9th August.
The Skybus fleet consists of Islanders GSBUS, GBUBN, GSSKY and two Twin-Otters GBIHO and GCBML. In addition to passengers, freight, mail and local produce are still carried. The journey to St. Mary's from Land's End takes around 15 minutes at about 1,500 feet. On busy Saturday's during the season as many as 45 round trips are made. Other routes that Skybus serves include Newquay, Exeter, Bristol and Southampton. The airlines base is still Land's End.

CHOXAWAY CAFÉ
The Choxaway Café was open seven days a week, 11 months of the year hummed with visitors from all over the world during the summer. You could listen to Pilots chatting about their flights while you tucked into a "Biggles Burger" or an "Aviator's Delight" - All-day-breakfast or Captain's Ruin" chocolate cake. Choxaway had lots of interesting pictures and model aeroplanes hung from the ceilings. A mural of two vintage aeroplanes covered one wall, and a pond, [formerly the holding tank for crayfish in the late 1960s]

"Choxaway" was always the heart of the airfield" stated David & Danielle Pitman. They would fly down from Bournemouth for weekends and always received a warm welcome, all day breakfast and a great selection of cakes for the trip home.

Following the departure of Rod Bellamy, Westward Airways reorganised their routes and ran a service to the Scilly Isles direct from Newquay and other airports. This reduced traffic at Lands End, and the Choxaway cafe was the first casualty. Ron and Rose, after much soul-searching, were forced to close operations and the great Choxaway Cafe disappeared. It had become a very expensive hobby. `Choxaway` ceased to be on October 31st 2004 [Apologies to `Monty Python`]

Engineering staff with Allison Yould (tech records) on right

Leslie Double, one of the hard working staff

A Bird's Eye View

Captain Peter Channon with Lesley Double.

Dave Gillard and Ron Tillotson, Bodmin

C.A.A. Visit to airfield and Cafe, October 2004
John Baker [2nd left]. Giles Hockin. Stephen Dench

Justus Hattam, a local visitor

55

Lands End Airfield

JOHN BOYNS

The late John Boyns love of flying endured until his demise in 2004. Flying Club member, Colin Brown referred to him as `a friend, curmudgeonly on the outside, with a depth of human understanding, rapier wit and encouragement to any that asked his opinions. His vast range of knowledge on a range of subjects helped to do the daily `crossy` seated in his favourite Lloyd loom chair, with a cup of disgustingly strong tea. One tea bag left in to stew and 4 lumps of sugar! His tobacco intake was legendary. His ability to function within in his own cloud probably stemmed from his navigation training in the RAF.

Image: Colin Brown, Frank the Fish and John Boynes

He joined up in 1938 and at the outbreak of World War 2, was a rear gunner in Hampden bombers. After completing a full tour of missions he was commissioned and trained as a navigator where he took part in the 1,000 bomber raids over Germany. One story he liked to tell was when he was `caught short` over Germany. `No toilet in those planes` he'd say, so he used one of the beautiful wooden boxes used to store valves for the wireless. – had lovely dovetailed joints`. Image: Colin Brown, Frank 'The Fish" and John Boyns"

However, having finished his business he dumped the box and contents out of the aircraft. Much to his chagrin he was fined seven shillings and sixpence for the loss of RAF property. In 1942 he was selected foe Pilot training in Canada. On graduating he was posted as a ferry pilot to India, his job to take replacement Hurricanes and Spitfires to various holes in the jungle where they were required to harness the retreating Japanese. Colin once asked him who picked him up to return to base. `Picked-up! ` he exploded, `I had to make my own way back sharpish – once in an ox-cart.` His ability to get the best out of people was reflected in his promotion to Squadron Leader and a permanent commission. He served until 1964 when he was diagnosed with terminal cancer. After the operation he was given 6 months to live, but John had other plans.

The Family purchased Levant House which they ran as a `B & B and campsite`. His love of flying, which had been curtailed on leaving the RAF was rekindled when one of his daughters, Jackie, who was fed up with her Dad being bored, suggested he join the Land`s End Flying Club, of which he soon became a popular member and with his two able `lieutenants` Geoff and Eric, used to take to the skies in their Cessna Oscar Delta.

A Bird's Eye View

Colin Brown became friends with John in the late 1980s when he was learning to fly. John was a constant source of encouragement to him and any `low-time` pilot, so was very pleased when asked to be his Safety Pilot towards the end of his flying career. He had a penchant for flying about 15 feet above the sea around the Brissoms then climbing to 6,000 feet because it was a nice day and it was his aircraft. He used to say that it was as close as he was likely to come to join the mile high club!

Colin can sometimes hear John saying: `Come on young Brown, you've been at it long enough – mine`s a tea, bag left in – 4 lumps. Get Oscar Delta out, I want to count the birds on the Brissoms`. `OK John`.

OCCASIONAL VISITORS

The helicopter from Penzance was an occasional visitor to the airfield, together with many GA aircraft from all over the UK and Europe.

57

Lands End Airfield

2005

In 2005 the Westward Airways fleet (Land's End Flying School) currently consisted of two Cessna 152's (G-OCPC and G-BFHT), a Cherokee 140 (G-ASPK) and the scenic Cessna FR 172F (GAWWU). The Club has operated as a Training School for over 30 years and taught PPL, NPPL, IMC and RTL courses.

Polly Vacher MBE, was 50 when she learned to fly. By the age of 60 she had flown solo around the World twice, landing on all seven continents. She also flew into Lands End on her epic Round the World flight. Image: Polly Vacher.

AIR TRAFFIC CONTROL

John Sharman used to fly to Lands End Airfield and go over to the Isles of Scilly where he checked out the Controllers. As he had relatives in West Cornwall, he stopped in Penzance.

John formerly spent 22 years in the R.A.F. flying approximately 5,000 hours and 60 types as QFI and Services test pilot. A spell as experimental pilot to industry, he then joined the Civil Air Traffic Control Services and resumed active flying as a Staff ATC inspector. He eventually retired from this second 20 year career and went on to become an ATC consultant. He donned an airline Captains hat flying Islanders until age regulations caught up with him. One of John's remarks was "I've changed horses so many times in midstream that most of them have drowned!

SATCO Ron Reilly provided the air Traffic control for this far-west sector and was affectionately known as "Popodom Leader . He managed the fly-past for the late Colin Shaw. All the Lands End fleet of planes was gathered into formation by him and flew past the church at Newlyn after the service.

Image: Chris Pearson, LND ATC

A Bird's Eye View

Nik Nicholas was an ATCO for many years at Lands End and whilst he was very helpful when he knew you, he occasionally got on the wrong side of some pilots. On one occasion Nick had instigated a new way of posting the day's forecast, by popping the sheet into a Tupperware pot and dropping it over the top of the control tower on a string. Someone from the Clubhouse below would have to come out, take it out of the container and pin it on the club wall. At the time Rod Bellamy's dog was not well and had left an ugly mound nearby. One of the pilots leaving the clubhouse scraped some of the dog's doings into the pot and stuck in a sign "the weather tomorrow is shitty". The system was quickly discontinued.

Nik could also be more than helpful. On various occasions a regular pilot from Bournemouth would ring up to check the weather and book in for arrival. He then received weather updates from ATO's in Exeter, Plymouth and St Mawgan as he passed en route - a service not heard of elsewhere.

By year 2000 there were three ATCOs at Land's End: Chris Pearson, Chris Wilkins and James Granger. Chris Pearson has been the longest serving ATCO of the three and as Air Traffic Manager was always brought up around Aviation, his Father, Bob Pearson, was previously a Controller at Land's End! Chris said, "I've always loved Cornwall – I've been coming down to the area with my family since I was a small child and when the chance came of a job at Land`s End, I knew I had to go for it. As a Controller you end up at many different Airports across the world, but with the view from the Control Tower looking over the Cornish coast-line with the Scilly Isles on the horizon – you can't but help thinking to yourself 'well, I've not done too badly here! `".

His first flight at the Airport- in 1981 was in an Islander in Westward colours - a Scenic Flight. He joined Westward Airways in October 1997 as a trainee ATCO. At that time the Instructors were Bill O 'Mahney, Nik Nicholas and Lori Williams. Chris Pearson was trained by Lori Williams who came from a busy Chichester Goodwood airfield. She then went north to an airport in Scotland, but returned later to Lands End to enjoy the Cornish atmosphere. Chris was promoted to Senior ATCO in April 2001 and then Airport Manager in April 2004.

Image: St Michaels Mount, Penzance

Image: The authors plane on a visit to the airfield

Lands End Airfield

The main customers were of course, Skybus and British International, but also included others, such as the locally based Land's End Flying Club, and Military Aircraft from RNAS Culdrose and RAF. St. Mawgan, Trinity House [the lighthouse operators], the Fishery Protection Fleet and of course the many visiting and local Private Pilots. There were a large number of pilots who looked forward each year in flying across the UK - and Europe to visit the area.

Equipment in the Tower included 2 main radio sets, a recording system that records every word from the Controllers and Pilots, Crash Alarms to alert the Emergency Services, a basic lighting system, a "strip-board" that keeps track of all Aircraft and vehicles, on & in the vicinity of the Aerodrome. One other critical piece of equipment was the kettle!

Currently, Land's End Airport ATCU is staffed by four ATCO's [all ADV, Met and OJTI rated]. Christopher Pearson as SATCO, Lori Williams, John Hudson and Ian Dewdney. They are employed by Westward Airways [Land's End] Ltd which is a subsidiary of parent Company – the Isles of Scilly Steamship Company. The parent Company also operates the ferry [Scillonian III] to the islands. The only other operator to the islands was British International Helicopters (Air Ground Service) using SK61's from Penzance Heliport site at Eastern Green, Penzance [which has just been sold to Sainsbury's]. They operated Monday to Saturday year round from approx 0800 to 1800 and handle approx 12,000 movements and 6,000 over-flights. The main [based] operator is 'Skybus' who conduct passenger/freight flights to the Isles of Scilly from us, Newquay, Exeter, Bristol and Southampton. Skybus operate the Britten Norman Islander (x3) and the De-Havilland Twin-Otter. Aircraft type is restricted by the runways on Scillies – longest being 600m.

THE DREADED FLUORESCENT JACKETS

Whilst there are many very active flying fields up and down the country that do not require fluorescent jackets to be worn air side, Lands End airfield issued a request to all pilots to wear them. This was a curious decision because visiting pilots simply did not and do not wear them from their planes to the club house, but were requested to wear them back.

On one occasion Shelia Trickey, the Chief Instructor asked where all the many club jackets had gone. Colin Brown, a long-standing flyer in his single-seater tail-dragger "Annie" mentioned that they were probably all in the hangar. Why asked Shelia: "Because I am obliged to wear one across to the hangar, then I take it off before flight and hang it on the wall. On returning I go straight from the hangar to the car - hence they are all in the hangar!" said Colin.

Image: Colin Brown in VP1 "Annie"

A Bird's Eye View

2009

Land's End Airport was temporarily closed during the afternoon of 28th January after a light aircraft, a four-seater, twin engine Diamond DA42 Twin Star aircraft, which was returning to Stapleford Airfield in Essex with three passengers on board, flipped over and landed on a hedge during take-off.

The passengers, a man and two teenaged boys, were cut free by St Just firemen, and suffered minor injuries in the accident which occurred shortly before 3pm. A bystander witnessed the accident from a near lay-by said: "It was taxiing down the runway and the engine wasn't sounding right. The next thing I knew there was a big cloud of dust or water come out of it and spray into the air and the plane just flipped completely over and went totally out of sight. The airport's fire and rescue service was on the scene within two minutes. Police and ambulance also attended. Jeff Marston, Managing Director of Westward Airways, which operates Land's End Airport, said: "Thankfully no-one was seriously injured and our emergency procedures worked extremely well." New fire truck at LEA 10th July 2009

2010 PRIVATE PLANES ASKED TO LEAVE

Approaching December 2010 all the members of the Lands End Flying Club were advised that the Club was not "viable" and was being closed by Westward Airways management. Those with aeroplanes on the field were asked to leave, and the planes were duly rolled out of the hangar.

At the time, members were informed that the hangar was to be used to house the Helicopter service based from Penzance, but this was not to happen. With some considerable upset, members flew away, many to Perranporth where there is a tarmac runway and a welcoming management and cafe.

Flying at Lands End was further curtailed with the restriction on flying from the field on Sundays, making it impossible for weekend flying visitors.

Image: empty hangars!

61

Lands End Airfield

G-OCPC, Pappa Charlie for short was one of the most popular planes in the South West. It had been the trainer for countless pilots and with arerobatic capability. It was often over Pendeen lighthouse performing Barrel Rolls, Lazy Eights, Loops and Tail Slides.

G-BOLX, Bollocks for short!
In 2009 the Club requested a plane that could be hired by members and could also be used for training. A Cessna Skyhawk was purchased and went into service. A few weeks later it was mentioned to the management just what a great name the plane had and they promptly got it changed.

TWITCHERS

Many of the passengers on their way to and from the Scillies were bird watchers. The Scillies was a great place for them to watch atlantic birds on their way North and South. The Airfield was also frequented by avid Bird-Watchers or `Twitchers` some of whom popped into the Café whilst awaiting news via bleeper/texts of rare bird sightings. The Choxaway 'Bird Log' was set up around 1998. Entries included: Little Egret flying over Carn Bran Farm Reserve, Gyr Falcon [from Greenland] at Carn Gloose Cape Cornwall, Baillons Crake, Collared Pratincole, Short-toed Lark, Spanish Wagtail, Chimney Swift and Cliff Swallow on St. Mary`1s, I.O.S. In 2001 Air Traffic Control reported `racing pigeons across airfield in front of my traffic!`. Tom Whitely could be spotted sketching birds seen locally - our `Beryl Cook`! One such sketch was displayed in the Café.

A Bird's Eye View

JULY 2012 WORK STARTS ON AIRPORT SCHEME

To enable the long-term future of L.E. Airport, the Isles of Scilly Steamship Company recently purchased the 90.4 acre site. Works began in late 2102 by demolishing the old building, to be replaced with a larger terminal with a new Control Tower. For much or 2012 the Control was run from a temporary unit and tower on the airfield.

During the late Autumn of 2012, rainfall across most of the UK became so intense that serious flooding ensued. Lands End field was also seriously affected with waterlogged runways. The Airport was closed for a long period that also coincided with the closure of the helicopter operations from Penzance, leaving the Scilly Isles residents short of services. On possible flying days, plane took off from Newquay and flew direct. By February 2013 new Terminal was complete and ready to commission, but not without some controversy, and continuing closure because of waterlogged runways. The previous tenants of the Lands End Cafe expected to move into the new terminal and continue their business serving dirnks and snacks to passengers. But they read in the local paper that the contract had been given to another operator from Newquay.

Image: On approach to land

Image: The Apron at Lands End

63

Lands End Airfield

THE LANDS END TRANSIT CORRIDOR

Lands End and St. Mary's ATC share the responsibility for the corridor and co-ordinate the traffic between one another. The radio transfer point between Lands End and St. Mary's is:

    a) VOR/DME - 10 DME from the LND VOR/DME (situated above Pendeen)
    b) GPS - 18nm from St. Mary's
    c) Visual Reference - Abeam Wolf Rock lighthouse on the S Boundary.

The Corridor can be a busy piece of airspace. It is not Controlled Airspace but a safe combination of vertical and horizontal separation is maintained between known aircraft within it. Commercial fixed-wing aircraft and helicopters are allocated levels from 500ft to 1500ft amsl, according to the wind direction. The upper limit of the corridor is 2000ft. If pilots prefer to make a crossing above this, they may be transferred to either Culdrose or Newquay for a radar service. As soon as a course is set, give your ETA to the ATCO so that it can be passed by Lands End ATC to St. Mary's or vice versa.

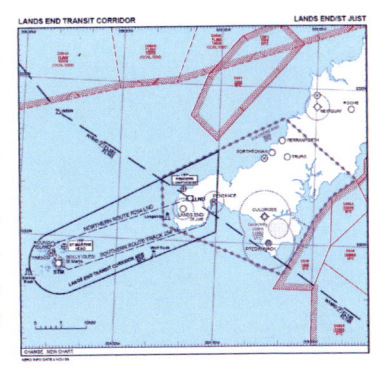

LANDS END VOR : LIMA NOVEMBER DELTA (LND)

Lima November Delta is a powerful radio beacon situated on the hill above Pendeen The transmitter, which looks like a flying saucer landing platform, can be seen from the main road. Known as a VOR, it transmits a powerful direction beacon, enabling aircraft to home in from the Atlantic, or other directions. All Atlantic pilots know the Lands End beacon very well.

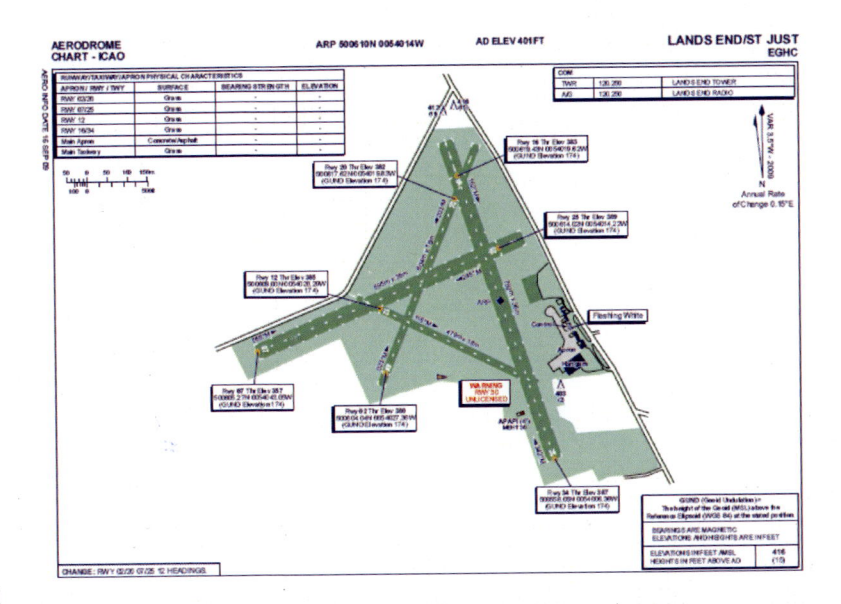

Lands End Airfield

During the War, services continued under Government controlled AAJC (Associated Airways Joint Committee) using Great Western & Southern Rapide Aircraft and crews. This continued until 1947, when BEA took over the AAJC Companies still operating the domestic flights in the United Kingdom.

At St. Mary's, I.O.S., a new landing ground, over-looking Old Town, was used for the first time on the 25th July 1939 – with runways of 667 yards and 593 yards.

By September, the Land`s End – St. Mary's Route had carried 10,000 passengers, 18,000 lbs of freight and 5000lbs of newspapers [since 1937]. Despite Government restrictions at the outbreak of War on 3rd September 1939, the Land`s End – St. Mary's route was considered important and therefore was allowed to continue.

The Staff were made aware that enemy agents might well try to travel to Scilly, so cameras were prohibited, and the cabin windows fitted with opaque material, to prevent passengers from looking out. Senior Service Personnel of ALL Forces, travelled on priority passes, but other passengers were also carried, so the Air Services proved a boon to Islanders, especially on days when the RMS Scillonian did not sail.

The Land`s End based De Havilland 84 Dragon and 89 Dragon Rapide spent several nights during the summer flying over Penzance and Truro as targets for local searchlight crews and were quickly camouflaged after War was declared. To avoid detection by the Germans, Service departure times were varied. Mainly at night, when not carrying passengers, the aircraft took part in Army cooperation exercises. Around this time the Army used a field on land belonging to Little Carn Grean Farm [opposite the airfield buildings] to house their bell tents. On the roadside down to Joppa Lane, dug-outs and trenches were constructed. The Enniskillen Fusiliers occupied the Land`s End Hotel.

1940

In the early 1940s, Egbert Rowe and his father Richard Henry [known as `Harry], of Tregerseal, St Just, were contracted by the Ministry – Board of Trade [owners of the airfield] had the contract to make new runways and re-seed them. In the process of this arduous task, Egbert wore out a chain-harrow! He was not allowed to `pilth` (burn rubbish) as it made too much smoke. Using their tractor to clear fields and level the ground. All the spoil was emptied towards the Pump-House adjacent to the Land`s End Road. A trench was made for a soak-a-way and Earthenware pipes were laid dovetail into the Pump-House. Jack Eddy's bulldozer was used to push earth and rock on land near Little Brea Vean.

A Bird's Eye View

There was an arrangement for the `Interchange` of tickets between GWS and the Isles of Scilly Steamship Company. Adult single airfare between Land`s End and Scilly was (old money) £1, and the return fare, £1.15s. 0d with half-price tickets for children aged 2–12 years. The rebated fare for Service Personnel was £1.11.6d. Boat fares were cheaper so corresponding financial adjustments were made when Air/Sea Travel Inter-change was necessary.

In those days, all passengers and baggage were weighed, and, passengers were seated according to individual weight. The heaviest were seated around the centre of gravity over the lower wing, and, the lightest, to the rear.

1938

In March a second Dragon G-ACPY was used on the route and a DH83 Fox Moth G-ACFF was made available for pleasure flights. From April onwards the service was increased to thrice daily with a Sunday service available on request. By May, a new service from Land's End to Plymouth had started. This then connected with flights to Bristol. The first recorded accident was on the 25th June. In very bad weather conditions that suddenly appeared at Land's End, G-ADCR crashed on landing. The six passengers were injured but recovered and the pilot Captain Dustin, sadly died. The Dragon aircraft was written-off.

By early December, Dragon G-ADDI replaced G-ADCR but on the 17th of December, G-ADDI failed to take-off and ended up in a Cornish granite hedge on the Sennen side of the airfield. The Pilot being slightly injured, the six passengers only shaken and the aircraft able to be repaired. At this time a group of glider enthusiasts flew occasionally from the beach at Penzance and a small airfield was opened at Ludgvan.

1939

By the spring of 1939 Channel Air Ferries had become Great Western and Southern Air Lines after nationalization of several British Airlines. Civil operations were cancelled at the outbreak of the Second World War, September 3rd. 1939, but resumed on 25th September 1939.

G-ADCR written off in bad weather on 25th June 1938. Captain Dustin was killed used for "joy-rides"

G-ADDI hit a Cornish hedge on 17th December 1938.

3

Lands End Airfield

Not only were there adders galore in the area, but also they were in abundance from Land's End to Bodmin! The Aerodrome quickly became known as Land's End.

Site preparation took until around June 1937. Approximately 400 tons of lime, thought to have been Plymouth Pink, was spread to combat the gorse and bracken growth, and to enhance the growth of grass. Dennis Manning also worked for Captain Gordon Olley, and, in the mid thirties delivered to St. Just Airfield from Squires Gate Aerodrome near Blackpool, an old asbestos and wooden framed hanger, covering 4,080 square feet. The hangar was re-erected by siblings, Ernest and Cedric Thomas and their friends.

DH 84 Rapide G-ADCR ready to go!

The first scheduled flight from Land's End took place on the 15th September 1937, using a de Havilland DH84 Dragon GADCR. There were four passengers and the pilot, Captain Dustin, a New Zealander and a little freight. It took off at 09:00 and landed at St. Mary's at 09:20. Five passengers, including the oldest resident on Scilly, Mr. John Mumford, who was going to visit his relatives in St. Just, made the return trip which departed at 09:50 and landed at 10:10. The fare was £1.0.0 single & £1.15.0 old money (£1.75) return. There was initially just the one flight a day in each direction. Tickets were interchangeable with those of the Isles of Scilly Steamship Company. A bus connected Penzance with the Aerodrome. This was timed to connect with the Cornish Riviera Express to Paddington.

The landing ground on St. Mary's, Isles of Scilly, was partially on the Golf Course (various hazards having been removed by the Club) and adjacent ground, with two landing runways: north-west/south-west of 430 yards and one at right angles of 455 yards. A Booking Office Hut was sited near the second green of the Golf Club. The site was staffed by four people: a traffic manager, his assistant, a porter and a boy complete with hand-bell to warn golfers of impending flights!

At Penzance, passengers were brought to the Airport by Western National bus from the Railway Station, but, only after the Bus Driver had checked by telephone with the airport office to find out if there were any delays caused by weather or mechanical problems. It was known for the Airport to be closed occasionally for several days, due to low cloud and fog, in which case the passengers were either transferred to the RMS Scillonian or went home!

DH Moth G-ACFF used for "joy-rides"

1930s

By the early 1930s commercial air transport was blossom[ing]. [In] 1929 the Penzance Road Transport Supervisor wrote to t[he Great] Western Railway, Sir Felix Pole, asking him to consider an air service connecting Penzance with Cardiff, with trips from Penzance to the Isles of Scilly. The suggestion was not taken up at that time. Since the early 1930s, a private airstrip had existed at St. Just serving the Porthledden Hotel, near the present Golf Club, but was not greatly used.

1936 THE START OF A FLYING DREAM.

When the land, once part of Trevegean Downs, located between Kelynack and Brea Downs, and a short distance south of the town of St. Just [-In-Penwith], in the beautiful far south-west of Cornwall, was purchased by Captain Gordon Olley from the Tregear Family in 1935, it was the start of his dream - one man's vision of an Airfield, linking the mainland to the Isles of Scilly. It comprised a flat plateau approximately 380 feet above sea level, adjacent to the B3306 St. Just to Land's End Road.

Captain Olley had visualized the possibility of a regular commercial air service from this flat grass field to the Isles of Scilly, only 28 miles away, and, on a clear day, easily visible from the aerodrome, just 15-20 minutes by plane. He already had the landing rights for a commercial Service between St. Mary's, Isles of Scilly and Penzance, inherited from his purchase of `Cobham Air Routes Ltd` from Sir Alan Cobham. Captain Olley registered a new airline "Channel Air Services" on the 8th May 1936, which would eventually operate from the St. Just Airfield with minimal facilities: a field with a landing range of 700 yards, one hangar, a Booking Office and a Fuel Store. DH89 G-ACYR was the first plane.

Managing and maintaining the site were the Pilots, Ground Engineers: Dick Trenary [from Sennen], Sim Withers, Jack Tregna and Tommy Hall [of Skewjack St. Levan] – cousin to Dr. Derrington. Tommy's brother Lawrence was employed as a Clerk, and, later (1943) went into the R.A.F. Sam Wells was employed as a wireless engineer.

1937

During this period, as well as making some `proving` flights in twin-engine Dragons, Gordon Olley employed the local St. Just Engineering Company, owned by the Thomas Brothers, to prepare the site. Cedric Thomas (his father Harvey, was later to become Captain of the M.V. Scillionan) and Gordon George, had the task of leveling the land. Scrub was cleared, great banks pushed away and pits filled in.

One of the tools they used was a Hodscraper/`Scuffler - a footed implement, manufactured at Holman's Foundry, St. Just. This was fitted to a Ferguson Tractor. St. Just Engineering Co. provided an old Austin 16, which, with the rear wheels removed, aided the extraction of the granite boulders.

Image: Old asbestos and wooden framed hanger

1